Fodor's InFocus

ZION &
BRYCE CANYON
NATIONAL PARKS

1st Edition

Where to Stay and Eat
for All Budgets

Must-See Sights
and Local Secrets

Ratings You Can Trust

Fodor's Travel Publications New York, Toronto, London, Sydney, Auckland
www.fodors.com

FODOR'S IN FOCUS ZION & BRYCE CANYON NATIONAL PARKS

Series Editor: Douglas Stallings
Editor: Douglas Stallings
Writer: Steve Pastorino

Editorial Contributors: Alexis Kelly, Laura Kidder
Editorial Production: Jennifer DePrima
Maps & Illustrations: David Lindroth and Mark Stroud, *cartographers*; Bob Blake and Rebecca Baer, *map editors*
Design: Fabrizio LaRocca, *creative director*; Guido Caroti, *art director*; Ann McBride, *designer*; Melanie Marin, *senior picture editor*
Cover Photo: Russ Bishop (Queen's Garden Trail, Bryce Canyon National Park, Utah)
Production/Manufacturing: Amanda Bullock

COPYRIGHT

1st Edition

ISBN 978-1-4000-0375-4

ISSN 1946-309X

SPECIAL SALES

This book is available for special discounts for bulk purchases for sales promotions or premiums. Special editions, including personalized covers, excerpts of existing books, and corporate imprints, can be created in large quantities for special needs. For more information, write to Special Markets/Premium Sales, 1745 Broadway, MD 6-2, New York, New York, NY 10019, or e-mail specialmarkets@randomhouse.com.

AN IMPORTANT TIP & AN INVITATION

Although all prices, opening times, and other details in this book are based on information supplied to us at press time, changes occur all the time in the travel world, and Fodor's cannot accept responsibility for facts that become outdated or for inadvertent errors or omissions. **So always confirm information when it matters,** especially if you're making a detour to visit a specific place. Your experiences—positive and negative—matter to us. If we have missed or misstated something, **please write to us.** We follow up on all suggestions. Contact the Zion & Bryce Canyon National Parks editor at editors@fodors.com or c/o Fodor's at 1745 Broadway, New York, NY 10019.

PRINTED IN THE UNITED STATES OF AMERICA
10 9 8 7 6 5 4 3 2 1

Be a Fodor's Correspondent

Your opinion matters. It matters to us. It matters to your fellow Fodor's travelers, too. And we'd like to hear it. In fact, we *need* to hear it. When you share your experiences and opinions, you become an active member of the Fodor's community. Here's how you can help improve Fodor's for all of us.

Tell us when we're right. We rely on local writers to give you an insider's perspective. But our writers and staff editors also depend on you. Your positive feedback is a vote to renew our recommendations for the next edition.

Tell us when we're wrong. We update most of our guides every year. But things change. If any of our descriptions are inaccurate or inadequate, we'll incorporate your changes in the next edition and will correct factual errors at fodors.com *immediately*.

Tell us what to include. You probably have had fantastic travel experiences that aren't yet in Fodor's. Why not share them with a community of like-minded travelers? Share your discoveries and experiences with everyone directly at fodors.com. Your input may lead us to add a new listing or a higher recommendation.

Give us your opinion instantly at our feedback center at www.fodors.com/feedback. You may also e-mail editors@fodors.com with the subject line "Zion & Bryce Canyon National Parks Editor." Or send your nominations, comments, and complaints by mail to Zion & Bryce Canyon National Parks Editor, Fodor's, 1745 Broadway, New York, NY 10019.

Happy Traveling!

Tim Jarrell, Publisher

CONTENTS

ABOUT THIS BOOK

Our Ratings

We wouldn't recommend a place that wasn't worth your time, but sometimes a place is so experiential that superlatives don't do it justice: you just have to be there to know. These sights, properties, and experiences get our highest rating, **Fodor's Choice**, indicated by orange stars throughout this book. Black stars highlight sights and properties we deem **Highly Recommended**, places that our writers, editors, and readers praise again and again for consistency and excellence.

Credit Cards

AE, D, DC, MC, V following restaurant and hotel listings indicate whether American Express, Discover, Diners Club, MasterCard, and Visa are accepted.

Restaurants

Unless we state otherwise, restaurants are open for lunch and dinner daily. We mention dress only when there's a specific requirement and reservations only when they're essential or not accepted.

Hotels

Unless we tell you otherwise, you can assume that the hotels have private bath, phone, TV, and air-conditioning. We always list facilities but not whether you'll be charged an extra fee to use them, so when pricing accommodations, find out what's included.

Many Listings
- ★ Fodor's Choice
- ★ Highly recommended
- ⊠ Physical address
- ✛ Directions
- ⌖ Mailing address
- ☎ Telephone
- 🖷 Fax
- ⊕ On the Web
- ✉ E-mail
- ⌨ Admission fee
- ☉ Open/closed times
- Ⓜ Metro stations
- ▤ Credit cards

Hotels & Restaurants
- ☶ Hotel
- ⇱ Number of rooms
- ⧖ Facilities
- ⵔ Meal plans
- ✕ Restaurant
- ⌑ Reservations
- ⭦ Smoking
- ⵙ BYOB
- ✕☶ Hotel with restaurant that warrants a visit

Outdoors
- ⚐ Golf
- ⚠ Camping

Other
- ♺ Family-friendly
- ⇨ See also
- ⊠ Branch address
- ☞ Take note

WHEN TO GO

Zion is the most heavily visited national park in Utah, receiving nearly 2.5 million visitors each year. Most visitors come between April and October, when upper Zion canyon is accessed only by free shuttle bus to reduce traffic congestion. Make your hotel reservations as far in advance as you can for this period of heaviest visitation. Although Zion Lodge is often booked solid, there are usually rooms in nearby Springdale, but at times you might have to travel as far as St. George to find lodging in the busiest days of summer.

Bryce is also most heavily visited between April and October, with July, August, and September the busiest three months. During these months, traffic on the main road can be crowded with cars following slow-moving RVs, so consider taking one of the park buses from the visitor center. Also in summer, lodging may be difficult to find since Bryce is more isolated than Zion. Winter offers more opportunities for solitude. The snow may be flying, but imagine the multi-hued rocks under an icing of white. Strap on snowshoes or cross-country skis, and you might just have a trail all to yourself.

Climate

Summer in Zion is hot and dry except for sudden cloudbursts, which can create flash flooding and spectacular waterfalls. Expect afternoon thunderstorms between July and September. But even in the height of summer, there is ample shade on the canyon floor. Winters are mild at lower desert elevations, so consider planning your visit for some time other than peak season. You can expect to encounter winter driving conditions from November through March, and although most park programs are suspended, winter is a wonderful and solitary time to see the canyons.

Around Bryce Canyon National Park and the nearby Cedar Breaks National Monument area, elevations approach and surpass 9,000 feet, making for temperamental weather, intermittent and seasonal road closures due to snow, and downright cold nights well into June. At this altitude, the warm summer sun is perfectly balanced by the coolness of the alpine forests during the day. Bryce gets much more snow than Zion, so keep that in mind when you plan a winter trip.

Welcome to Zion & Bryce Canyon

WORD OF MOUTH

"One hint: Remember in Zion one looks 'up,' while in Bryce one looks 'down.' You'll see what I mean when you are there. And be sure to do Zion first."
—Castleblanca

By Steve
Pastorino

LOOK UP, LOOK DOWN. REPEAT—AS MANY TIMES AS NECESSARY. As much as any national park in America, Bryce Canyon and Zion are truly "vertical" experiences that challenge your senses with chasms and towers galore. Two key steps in the Giant Staircase—the geological phenomenon that stretches from the Grand Canyon (the floor of which is near sea level) to Bryce's Paunsaugunt Plateau (9,115 feet above sea level)—these brilliant places are just a small section of a massive Southwest puzzle where geologists are still unlocking the secrets to a billion years of the planet's history from the predinosaur eras to the present.

Standing at the base of 2,000 feet of sheer rock in Zion's Virgin River Canyon, feel the cool canyon breezes that have attracted human exploration for thousands of years. Even on summer's hottest days, cottonwoods rustle, and dozens of birds and mammals congregate in this "place of sanctuary" that provides a respite from searing desert heat. Nineteenth-century settlers were so astounded by Zion's wonders that they turned to their most revered text, the Bible, to find names for formations like the Three Patriarchs (Abraham, Jacob, and Isaac).

Because Zion has now become one of the most visited parks in America, the decision to ban cars from the canyon's heart a decade ago has had only positive ramifications—cleaning the air, unclogging the roads, and encouraging guests to ride an efficient shuttle service with nothing to worry about but their own enjoyment of the setting. An array of trails, interpretive exhibits, and learning experiences awaits visitors of all ages. More ambitious explorers plan months, if not years, to hike two of America's most renowned hikes, the Narrows and Subway. Either hike can be enjoyed in a half-day "from the bottom up" jaunt, or as a rigorous backcountry overnight trek. On the eastern side of the park, no visitor should miss the Zion–Mt. Carmel drive, which climbs thousands of feet adjacent to the Grand Arch. Then it disappears into a mile-long tunnel that is no less an engineering wonder today than when it was blasted out of the rock 80 years ago. By the way, the Checkerboard Mesa landscape that awaits you on the park's east side is a geological wonder in its own right.

A few thousand feet higher toward the sky and less than 50 mi to the north, Bryce Canyon is a celebration of visitor-friendly geology that every high school science teacher must be thankful for. Hoodoos, spires, canyons, and amphitheaters are the superstars of this park. Join a ranger tour, watch the visitor center's film, and hop out of your vehicle throughout this long, narrow park to gain an appreciation for its magic. Here, forces of nature (erosion, freezing, thawing, and wind) have created fanciful formations like Thor's Hammer, Queen Victoria, and Wall Street. Bryce may not have as many hikes or mammals as some national parks, but arches, natural bridges, and hundreds of species of birds more than make up for the smaller variety of mammals and reptiles.

Many park visitors combine Zion and Bryce with a visit to the Grand Canyon or Las Vegas, but don't sell southern Utah short. Combined with three nearby national monuments (Cedar Breaks, Pipe Springs, and the sprawling Grand Staircase–Escalante), three other nearby national parks, a bevy of dinosaur excavation sites, a renowned summer Shakespeare festival in Cedar City, and affordable skiing at Brian Head in winter, you can easily spend a week here.

HISTORY OF THE PARKS

ZION NATIONAL PARK

Break out the champagne and cake: Zion National Park is celebrating its 100th anniversary in 2009. The park was founded in 1909 as Mukuntuweap National Monument. Ten years later, Zion became the first of Utah's five national parks.

Zion Canyon has a much longer human history than Bryce. There's evidence of human settlements in the lush, cool delta of the Virgin River as early as 500 AD when the Virgin Anasazi and Parowan Fremont created year-round communities, cultivated crops, and utilized ceramic vessels. Here, bow and arrow use became widespread.

But both civilizations disappear from archaeological records about 1300 AD, apparently victims of massive droughts and intermittent catastrophic flooding. The mobile Southern Paiute Indians appear to have filled the void in Zion for some of the ensuing 500 years, before Euro-American explorations began to crisscross the Southwest on the Old Spanish Trail.

CLOSE UP   Most-Visited National Parks (2007)

There may be a few less-visited parks in the western U.S., but Zion is not among them. While it is not in the same league as the most-visited parks (Great Smoky Mountains, Grand Canyon, and Yosemite), it does rank in the top seven.

1. Great Smoky Mountains NP: 9,289,215
2. Grand Canyon NP: 4,279,439
3. Yosemite NP: 3,242,644
4. Yellowstone NP: 2,870,295
5. Olympic NP: 2,749,197
6. Rocky Mountain NP: 2,743,676
7. Zion NP: 2,567,350

Brigham Young's Church of Latter Day Saints descended on the Salt Lake Valley (approximately 300 mi to the north) in 1847, and by 1863, Isaac Behunin built the first log cabin in Zion Canyon. Behunin, clearly full of religious fervor, is credited with naming Zion. Mormon scouts and settlers added many of the religion-suffused names such as the Three Patriarchs, Great White Throne, Angel's Landing, and at least three temples (East, West, and Sinawava).

In 1909 Mukuntuweap National Monument was established despite poor roads and distant railroad stations. It was virtually inaccessible to the public. Aggressive promotion, politicking, and development by the Union Pacific Railroad slowly improved the access to southern Utah—an important tourism destination on the railroad's dominant western network.

After the government granted national park status to Zion in 1919, visitation steadily grew. Union Pacific commissioned Gilbert Stanley Underwood to build the Zion Lodge. The construction of the Zion–Mt. Carmel Highway in 1930 significantly shortened travel times throughout the Southwest and created the traffic that still makes Zion one of the most-visited national parks in America.

CLOSE UP | Zion's Centennial Celebration

In 2009 Zion National Park will celebrate the 100th anniversary of its founding. Activities take place all year long, including the following:

■ Lecture Series: October 8, 2008 through February 9, 2009

■ Special Utah License Plate: throughout 2009

■ Special Exhibits in Human History Museum: throughout 2009

■ Special Interpretive Programs: throughout high season

■ Zion Field Institute Classes with Historical Themes: March, April, October 2009

■ Film Series of Movies filmed in and near Zion National Park: June through August 2009

■ "Vision of Zion" Kids Art Show: June 23 through August 3, 2009

■ 100th Anniversary Ceremony: July 31, 2009

BRYCE CANYON

First designated a national monument in 1923, Bryce Canyon was officially established as a national park in 1928, nine years after Zion gained the same status. In addition to being inexorably connected in a "Grand Circle" of Southwestern natural monuments, Zion and Bryce Canyon were once jointly managed and have been linked since Bryce's earliest days.

According to National Park Service documents, it was not until after the Civil War that Bryce Canyon began to wriggle its way into America's consciousness. Captain James Andrus may have seen its cliffs in 1866 when he set out from St. George to pursue "marauding" Navajo Indians. Six years later, Grove Karl Gilbert wrote of "a perfect wilderness, the stunningest thing out of a picture." His words, along with sketches by John Weyss and increased Mormon settlement across the southern half of the state, attracted the interest of writers, artists, and traders.

When J.H. Humphrey became a National Park Service supervisor in 1915, extensive explorations of the Paunsaugunt Plateau began—and rail barons took notice. Union Pacific Railroad officials saw Bryce as a key link for their growing Grand Canyon North Rim business, which had a longer tourism season than Yellowstone, its signature attraction at the time.

In 1927 Union Pacific and the National Park Service negotiated an historic swap. In exchange for more than 11 acres at Bryce Canyon that consolidated the park entrance, the park service agreed to build the Zion–Mt. Carmel tunnel in Zion National Park. The road significantly reduced travel times through Zion to the Grand Canyon, where Union Pacific operated rail service and desired to expand hotels and services. Union Pacific also received rights to build Bryce Canyon Lodge, a perfect match for the railroad's concessions in Zion and Grand Canyon—and a critical component in the development of the Grand Circle.

What resulted is the protection and preservation of what Bryce historian Nicholas Scrattish called "one of the world's best sites for an appreciation of the inexorable, titanic forces which have shaped the globe's surface."

WHO WAS EBENEZER BRYCE? The park is named for Mormon settler Ebenezer Bryce, who settled just south of the current community of Cannonville in 1875. Bryce dug an irrigation ditch for farming and a road to haul timber and common staples. Reports say the road ended at the base of the canyon, which was dubbed "Bryce's Canyon." Ironically, Ebenezer was not quite as awed by the canyons as others—he moved his family to Arizona in 1880. The name, obviously, stayed around.

GEOLOGY OF THE PARKS

To understand the geology of Bryce and Zion canyons, begin with the Grand Staircase. It spans more than 150 mi, from the Paunsaugunt Plateau of Bryce Canyon (Yovimpa Point is 9,100 feet above sea level) to the south rim of the Grand Canyon (6,800 feet). Deep canyons slice through the Grand Staircase, creating some locations that are only nominally above sea level.

Bryce sits on top as the youngest sibling. Its oldest layers are a mere 65 million years old, formed in an era dominated by a massive inland lake. Bryce is characterized by a series of amphitheaters cut into the Paunsaugunt plateau. Erosion and frost-wedging (the frequent freezing and thawing of moisture in rocks) has shaped the multihued rock into the canyons, arches, and spires you see today. Bryce Canyon's famous hoodoos are in Pink Cliffs layer, so named for the combination of limestone, mudstone, and sandstone sediments, plus unique mineral deposits that cast the rock in trademark reddish tint. Gray, white, vermilion, and chocolate cliffs define the steps "down" to the Grand Canyon.

Zion Canyon is one of the middle siblings. Its oldest layers date back 240 million years to an arid era that turned the region into a massive blown-sand desert 3,000 feet deep. Zion is in the White Cliffs layer, as clearly evidenced by the moonlike topography of Checkerboard Mesa and the 2,400-foot deep Temple of Sinawava. Zion was once a relatively flat basin near sea level, but sand, gravel, and mud eroded from nearby mountains depositing, over time, 10,000 feet of material. Where the material is harder, the Virgin River's erosion is slow-going, resulting in deep, slender gorges like the Narrows. When the river finds a softer Kayenta formation (as it does at the mouth of the canyon), it cuts away at the shale more rapidly, causing it to fall away from the cliffs and widen the canyon.

Farther south, the Grand Canyon has some of the oldest exposed rock in the world; some of the sedimentary rock there is more than 1,000 million old. Geologists, paleontologists, and archaeologists flock to the Grand Staircase region because it preserves so much of the planet's history in visible, accessible proximity. Within and surrounding the nearby Grand Staircase–Escalante National Monument are hundreds of formations, slot canyons, dinosaur excavation sites, and Native American hieroglyphics.

FLORA & FAUNA

With elevations ranging from 3,600 to 9,100 feet, Zion and Bryce Canyon offer a multitude of plant environments and species. The contrast is stark between the deserts and slickrock to cool, deep canyons, hanging gardens, and high plateaus.

FLORA

Bristlecone pine (*Pinus longaeva*): These are some of the oldest living organisms on earth. The oldest one in Bryce Canyon (at Yovimpa Point) is estimated to be more than 1,600 years old. You can see bristlecone pine trees on the Fairyland Loop trail, the Bristlecone Loop trail, on the Peek-a-Boo Trail, and in places along the Rim Trail near Inspiration Point. As exposed root systems may die in portions, the remaining living parts of the tree may adopt a twisted, tortured look.

Park Passes

An annual pass, available for $50, gives unlimited access to Zion National Park. Bryce Canyon's annual pass is $30. If you plan to visit several national parks, one of the best available values is the America the Beautiful–National Parks and Recreational Lands Pass (☎ 888/275-8747 Ext. 1 ⊕ store. usgs.gov/pass), available for $80, which gives unlimited access to all federal recreation areas and national parks for 12 months from the purchase date. The America the Beautiful Senior Pass has the same benefits for U.S. citizens age 62 or older for the cost of $10.

Both parks charge $25 for a seven-day pass for a private vehicle. Otherwise, it's $12 per person for pedestrians, bicyclists, motorcycle, or organized groups.

Fremont cottonwood (*Populus fremontii*): The presence of these trees indicates a long-term water source—look for them along the Virgin River in Zion National Park. Younger trees have smooth bark; older ones develop deeply furrowed, whitish cracked bark.

Juniper: Two species of juniper predominate in this region. *Juniperus osteosperma* (found only in Utah) and *Juniperus scopulorum* (found throughout the Rocky Mountain region) grow in both Bryce and Zion. The Rocky Mountain variety grows tall and thin in cool, shady areas. Utah Junipers are found at lower elevations. Both are characterized by blueberry-shaped cones that are used for flavoring gin and were used by Native Americans for medicinal and ceremonial purposes.

Limber pine (*Pinus flexilis*): The durable limber pine grows near timberline, from 5,000 to 12,000 feet. It's only found growing in places where competing species (such as white fir, Douglas Fir, and Engelmann spruce) can't survive, which often means southwestern slopes, on the very edges of cliffs, or in pockets on talus slopes. This pine has a short, thick trunk with an irregular crown and can develop a stunted, twisted form.

Oaks: *Quercus gambelii* (the common gambel oak) and *Quercus turbinella* (the shrub oak) are common in Bryce and Zion. These trees survive with root systems that can grow 35 feet deep and 16 feet wide in order to maximize access to moisture.

Ponderosa pine (*Pinus albicaulis*): You can easily identify ponderosa pine by the tall, straight trunks, which have a reddish-orange, puzzle-piece-shaped bark that smells like vanilla. Named for the heavy "ponderous" wood, they are visible throughout Bryce Canyon and Zion national parks.

Quaking aspen (*Populus tremuloides*): Look for quaking aspen on level, moist ground as well as on dry slopes. The bark of these trees is smooth; they get their name from the leaves, which seem to quiver in a light breeze.

Resurrection moss (*Selaginella family*): Commonly found on many rock faces and boulders, this moss lies dark and essentially dormant until it comes in contact with water (in the form of rain or a hiker's bottle). Then it springs to life, doubling in size, turning green, and absorbing the liquid like a sponge. Look for it and dribble some water on it!

Rock columbine (*Aquilegia scopulorum*): The blue flowers contrast with the red cliffs and soil of Bryce Canyon and are some of the more distinctive plants in the park. Highly regarded for their beauty, columbines have been used for ornamentation and perfumes for centuries.

Sagebrush: As is the case throughout much of Wyoming, Montana, Utah, Idaho, and Nevada, the high plateaus of Bryce and Zion feature sagebrush (*Artemisia tridentate*) and wild grasses such as Pacific fescue (*Festuca pacifica*).

FAUNA

Hundreds of species of birds and dozens of mammals, reptiles, and amphibians make their homes in Bryce and Zion national parks. The parks are an ornithologist's delight, with some of America's rarest wild birds (California condors) sharing habitats with some of nature's most energetic small birds (American dipper and Stellar's jay). Camera-wielding mammal hunters may be rewarded with the sight of desert bighorn sheep, mule deer, and pronghorn. Sightings of mountain lions and even an occasional black bear (in Zion) are extremely rare, although both larger mammals certainly inhabit the parks.

BIRDS

California condor (*Gymnogyps californianus*): The largest bird of prey in North America was extinct in the wild as recently as 1992. Reintroduced in California and Arizona, a few have found their way to Zion National Park. Spotted on the cliffs near Kolob Terrace Road in 2008, they are nonetheless an extremely rare sight. Twice as large as turkey vultures, they have wingspans as long as nine feet and white "armpits" on their dark plumage.

Clark's nutcracker (*Nucifraga columbiana*): Named for William Clark (of the Lewis & Clark Expedition), Clark's nutcrackers are gray-and-black birds found throughout Bryce Canyon. They feed on the nuts from pinyon, limber, and whiteback pines—and also store tens of thousands of nuts in the ground, which facilitates the sprouting of new trees.

Peregrine falcon (*Falco peregrinus*): With wingspans more than 3 feet wide, these falcons are often spotted near their nesting sites along cliffs and rocky ledges. These aerial acrobats are monogamous and mate for life. Look for them in quieter, southern portions of Bryce Canyon along with the Fairyland Point area.

Stellar's jay (*Cyanocitta stelleri*): It's hard to miss these bold blue and black birds. Found throughout both parks, they have harsh voices, sharp crests, and solitary behavior (unlike common blue jays).

Water ouzel (*Cinclus mexicanus*): Commonly know as the "American dipper," this aquatic songbird is seen (and heard) by Zion's rivers. It stands alongside shallow streams and constantly dips its head in the water to find food.

Wild turkey (*Meleagris gallopavo*): On a Zion bus tour at dusk, an alert guide may point out flocks of turkey as looming silhouettes in the trees above the park road. Look for colorful heads and dark bodies that may have white tips on their rich plumage.

FISH, REPTILES & AMPHIBIANS

Great Basin rattlesnake (*Crotalus viridis lutosus*): One of the parks' most famous and feared inhabitants, the rattlesnake, sits and waits for its prey to approach. The snakes have excellent eyesight and aim and can also sense approaching animals via vibrations in the ground. Stay on trails to avoid an unexpected encounter—and if bitten, seek medical attention immediately. Rattlesnake bites are seldom fatal but do require immediate treatment.

Whiptail lizard (*Cnemidophorus tigris*): These long, slender lizards are named for the way their tails swish from side to side while running. Extremely common to Zion, they're equally likely to be found in desert scrub, grasslands, and pine forests. There are a dozen other varieties of lizards in both parks. Tiny ones will dart across your path around the lodges, visitor centers, and campsites. If you're lucky, you may come across the distinctive **collared lizard** (*Crotaphytus collaris*), which has distinctive stripes across the back of its neck making it look as if it is wearing a collar.

Zion snail (*Physella zionis*): Invisible to the naked eye, the Zion snail is nonetheless one of the most famous park inhabitants. The microscopic snails are a unique variety found nowhere else in the world. Scientists tell us they live below the Hanging Gardens of Orderville and Virgin River canyons, including the famous Narrows.

MAMMALS

Bighorn sheep (*Ovis canadensis*): Look for the rams (male) and ewes (female) in the Checkerboard Mesa area of Zion. With their keen eyesight, odds are they will see you first. The hollow-horned animals are especially active in fall. With padded hooves, they are uniquely suited to the steep, rocky slopes and canyons of the park.

Coyote (*Canis latrans*): Smaller, but otherwise similar in shape and coloring to gray wolves, coyotes are found in every state in America, so it's no surprise that they wander through Bryce and Zion. These extremely intelligent canines are omnivores, chasing down everything from rodents to weakened bighorns and pronghorns. Look for them in park grasslands and meadows, particularly around dawn and dusk.

Foxes: Three species of fox are found in Zion—the gray fox (*Urocyon cinereoargenteus*), red fox (*Vulpes vulpes*), and kit fox (*Vulpes macrotis*). Look for them in park grasslands and meadows, particularly around dawn and dusk.

Mountain lion (*Felis concolor*): Also known as cougars, these predators are rarely seen by humans in Zion and Bryce and live almost exclusively in the remote backcountry. Their

Bringing Your Pet

Most national parks are not particularly pet-friendly. In both Zion and Bryce, pets are not allowed in the backcountry, on trails, at viewpoints, or in buildings.

There is only one exception to the "no pets on the trail" rule, and that is the Pa'rus Trail in Zion, a flat, paved trail near the park entrance. Even here, you may wish to think twice as the trail is also used by bicyclists, who may distract your animal

But think twice before bringing your pet to either park. Where will Rover stay while you roam

the park trails? The summer heat in Zion can be a huge issue for your pet's safety. Dogs are allowed in campgrounds, but they must be on a leash anytime they are outside; pets are not allowed in any of the other accommodations in the park, nor are they allowed on the shuttle (except for service animals).

There are private kennels in Rockville, Hurricane, Kanab, St. George, and Cedar City where you can board your pet while you explore Zion and Bryce national parks.

---

primary prey includes deer and smaller mammals, but they have been known to attack elk as well.

Pronghorn antelope (*Antilocapra americanus*): With a sprint that appears almost effortless as it bounds across meadows of the high plateau of Bryce Canyon, the pronghorns are a beautiful sight to behold.

Utah prairie dog (*Cynomys parvidens*): This cuddly looking creature should be enjoyed from afar. The Utah species has only recently recovered from endangered status, and they're known to carry diseases that could transfer to humans in the event of an accidental bite.

IF YOU LIKE . . .

ROCKS

Zion and Bryce offer an up-close look at 240 million years of geological history in an enchanting, breathtaking setting. You'll be hard-pressed to find hoodoos like Bryce's anywhere on the planet. And the humility (and humanity) you sense below Zion's 2,000-foot cliffs can be humbling.

1

PEERING DOWN FROM ON HIGH

Whether you're at Angel's Landing (Zion) or Bryce Point (Bryce), brace yourself as you peek down 1,000 feet of vertigo-inducing cliffs. You have to earn the views at Zion, where the ascents sometimes feel like you're headed straight up the side of a cliff. At Bryce, many great vistas are only a few steps from your car.

EXPLORING IN YOUR CAR

The Zion–Mt. Carmel road (not to mention the tunnel) is one of the signature drives in the national park system. But Kolob Canyon Road, also in Zion, is a journey in its own right, as is the 36-mi round-trip through Bryce Canyon. It's hard to visit either park without spending some time on Highway 89 or 12; each is a local treasure leading to countless sights.

STARGAZING

The benefit of these parks' remote locations is a stargazing experience that is about as good as you can possibly get in the United States. Both parks offer late-night stargazing hikes where rangers point out the obvious (the Milky Way glows here) and the not-so-obvious (planets, astrological signs, satellites, and more).

EASY CAMPING

Campgrounds at both parks are a few miles (or yards in the case of Watchman in Zion) from visitor centers, grocery stores, and other amenities your children might think they can't live without. All campgrounds in both parks have bathrooms, potable water, fire pits, and picnic tables, as well as space for RVs and groups. For a quieter experience, ask about backcountry camping, but be prepared for the polar opposite—no amenities other than a clearing in some cases.

FAMILY FUN

National parks are great family destinations, and Zion and Bryce Canyon are no exceptions. Before you even arrive at the park, kids can explore the parks' Web sites as "virtual rangers." Once you arrive at the park, Junior Ranger newspapers offer creative and fun ways for kids to enjoy the park—from wildlife-watching to meeting and learning from park rangers.

CLOSE UP

Tips for RVers

The single most important consideration for traveling to Bryce and Zion is the ban on large vehicles on the Zion–Mt. Carmel Highway. This eastern entrance (or exit) to Zion crosses through an 80-year-old, mile-long tunnel that is too small for many contemporary RVs.

Vehicles taller than 13 feet, 1 inch, longer than 40 feet, or more than 50,000 pounds are prohibited, as well as commercial trucks, any vehicle carrying hazardous materials, bicycles, and pedestrians. Vehicles towing a trailer with a combined length of 50 feet are also prohibited.

Vehicles sized at least 7 feet, 10 inches in width, or 11 feet, 4 inches in height will require an escort and a fee of $15. Each fee is good for two trips through the tunnel during a seven-day period. Nearly every RV, bus, trailer, dual-wheel truck, and boat trailer will require an escort. Measurements include mirrors, awnings, rear-mounted tires, etc.

Once inside either park, there are no full-service hookups in any of the campgrounds. Pull-through sites and dump stations are available, however. All four campgrounds in the two parks welcome RVs, but check the individual park Web sites or call ahead for site availability.

From March through October, sites at Zion's Watchman campground can be reserved six months in advance (⊕www.recreation.gov). Otherwise they are first-come, first-served. South Campground is open from May through early November only and is always first-come, first-served.

In Bryce, sites in the North campground can be reserved 240 days in advance of the summer season from May through September (⊕www.recreation.gov) and are available on a first-come, first-served basis otherwise. Sunset Campground is open from late spring to early fall, depending on weather conditions.

Campgrounds with full hookups are available just outside both parks and throughout the surrounding region.

IN ZION

Even small children seem to appreciate Zion's towering cliffs. Ride the shuttle throughout the park, and pick several spots in Zion Canyon to explore on foot. Weeping Rock is a perfect short hike for little ones, and many teens will derive a great sense of satisfaction from climbing Angel's Landing. In summer, anyone can wander the Riverside Walk. Be prepared for the kids to want to splash in the Virgin River even if you don't hike upriver toward the Narrows. Zion's campgrounds are especially kid-friendly, with the paved Pa'rus trail a great spot to walk the family dog (about the only place in the park where pets are welcome) and ride bicycles.

Just outside the park, the Zion Giant Screen Theater shows park-themed movies as well as at least one family-friendly general release film. Although the traffic can get busy, Springdale offers many places to wander, shop, and grab a snack or meal. Many hotels have swimming pools, and outfitters like Zion Adventure Co. can arrange bike rides, ATV explorations, family-oriented canyoneering trips, and much more—just not inside the national park.

BRYCE CANYON

You've undoubtedly had to drive some distance to arrive at Bryce Canyon, and for many people the park is experienced as a scenic drive. For the kids' sake, get out of the car and enjoy some of the park on foot as well. Great short hikes include Mossy Cave and the Rim Trail from Sunrise Point to Sunset Point. Kids will appreciate the hoodoos more if they can see them up close, so explore Navajo Loop and/or Queen's Garden—just remember that a taxing ascent awaits after you drop down into the canyon.

If you have the better part of a day, sign preteens up for the Junior Ranger program at the visitor center. The park will become a giant scavenger hunt for them. Junior Rangers are required to participate in a Ranger-led activity (a hike, talk, campfire, etc.), and the programs are always well tailored for both adults and kids. Also, look for deer, prairie dogs, and other mammals in the meadows adjacent to the park roads; and listen for songbirds, owls, and hundreds of other bird species. Be sure to stay a night, or at least wander through the historic lodge (it's on the

National Register of Historic Places) and enjoy a meal (kids' menu available).

Finally, Ruby's Inn—right at the park entrance—offers an array of kids' activities from horseback rides to a rodeo in summer, plus an "Old West" shopping area, swimming pools, hand-dipped ice-cream parlor, and much more.

Exploring Zion

2

WORD OF MOUTH

"You will really need to prioritize your time at Zion because it's big."

—Carolv

www.fodors.com/forums

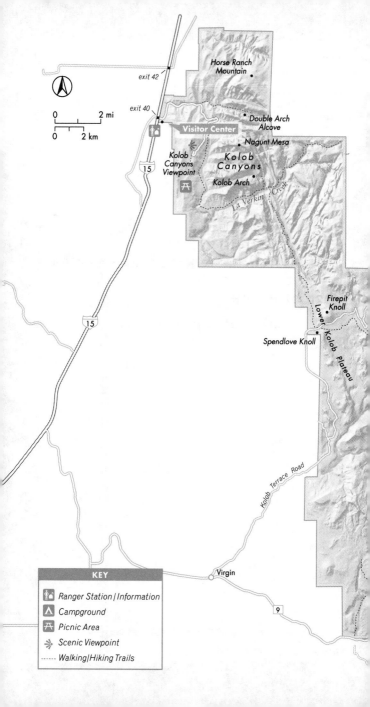

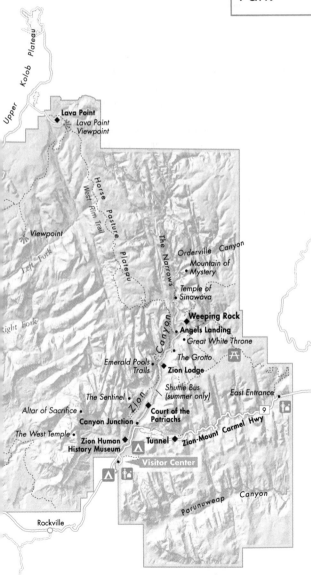

Zion National Park

Upper
Kolob Plateau

Lava Point
Lava Point Viewpoint

Horse Pasture Plateau

West Rim Trail

The Narrows

Viewpoint

Left Fork

Right Fork

Orderville Canyon

Mountain of
• Mystery

Temple of
• Sinawava

Weeping Rock

• Angels Landing

• Great White Throne

Emerald Pools
Trails

• The Grotto

Zion Lodge

*Shuttle Bus
(summer only)*

The Sentinel

Altar of Sacrifice •

Canyon Junction

**Court of the
Patriachs**

East Entrance

9

Zion-Mount Carmel Hwy

The West Temple

**Zion Human
History Museum**

Tunnel ◆ **Zion-Mount Carmel Hwy**

Visitor Center

Parunuweap Canyon

Rockville

By Steve
Pastorino

THE WALLS OF ZION CANYON SOAR more than 2,000 feet above the valley below, but it's the character, not the size, of the sandstone forms that defines the park's splendor. The domes, fins, and blocky massifs bear the names and likenesses of cathedrals and temples, prophets and angels. But for all Zion's grandeur, trails that lead deep into side canyons and up narrow ledges on the sheer canyon walls reveal a subtler beauty. Tucked among the monoliths are delicate hanging gardens, serene spring-fed pools, and shaded spots of solitude. So diverse is this place that 85% of Utah's flora and fauna species are found here. Some, like the tiny Zion snail, appear nowhere else in the world.

At the genesis of Zion is the Virgin River, a tributary of the mighty Colorado. It's hard to believe that this muddy little stream is responsible for carving the great canyon you see, until you witness it transformed into a rumbling red torrent during spring runoff and summer thunderstorms. Cascades pour from the cliff tops, clouds float through the canyon, and then the sun comes out and you know you're walking in one of the West's most loved and sacred places. If you're lucky, you may catch such a spectacle, but when the noisy waters run thick with debris, make sure that you keep a safe distance—these "flash floods" can, and do, kill.

The park comprises two distinct sections—Zion Canyon, and the Kolob Plateau and Canyons. Most people restrict their visit to the better-known Zion Canyon, especially if they have only one day to explore, but the Kolob area has much to offer and should not be missed if time allows. There's little evidence of Kolob's beauty from the entrance point off Interstate 15, but once you negotiate the first switchback on the park road, you are hit with a vision of red rock cliffs shooting out of the earth. As you climb in elevation you are treated first to a journey through these canyons, then with a view into the chasm. Due to geography—no roads connect Zion Canyon with Kolob Canyon—and to access points that are far apart, it is difficult to explore both sections in one day.

PLANNING YOUR TIME

ZION IN ONE DAY

Begin your visit at the **Zion Canyon Visitor Center,** where outdoor exhibits inform you about the park's geology, wildlife, history, and trails. Plan to spend some time with a ranger—the programs are concise, informative, and family-friendly.

ZION BEST BETS

■ **Zion Canyon:** The heart of the park for many visitors, the meadows, cool canyon breezes, and shady cottonwoods have a just reputation as a place of sanctuary since pre-Columbian times.

■ **The Great Arch:** It forms an enchanting backdrop as you drive the Zion–Mt. Carmel Highway to the east side of the park. Don't miss the Canyon Overlook viewpoint atop the arch.

■ **A millennium of human history:** As displayed at the Human History Museum, the baskets, ceramics, and village remnants found here indicate that the Virgin Anasazi considered this place special long before white settlers arrived in the 19th century.

■ **The Narrows:** The canyons are feet from wall to wall—and 2,000 feet up to the sky. A hike through water is the only way to get here!

■ **Kolob Canyons:** Barely 10% of park visitors find this corner of the park. Its visitor center is a few yards off I-15, and stunning "finger" canyons await you.

Catch the shuttle or drive—depending on the season—into Zion Canyon. On your way in, make a quick stop at the **Zion Human History Museum** to watch a 22-minute park orientation program and to see exhibits chronicling the human history of the area.

Since you can't do it all in one day, pick at least one "signature" hike to gain a better appreciation of the park. Allow three to four hours for the **Angel's Landing Trail,** or two hours to reach the Upper Pool on the **Emerald Pools Trail.** Then relax and recover with a shuttle ride (in summer) to the last stop, Temple of Sinawava, where you can tip your toes in the Virgin River on the paved, accessible **Riverside Walk.** Conditions permitting, wander upstream for as far as 5 mi. (Wear boots and consider a walking stick if you hike in the river.)

As you work your way back to the visitor center, make brief stops at **Weeping Rock** and **Zion Lodge** to see the historic hotel and/or to grab some refreshments.

Save an hour for the **Zion–Mt. Carmel Highway,** a winding, climbing drive to the park's east entrance. Keep your camera handy for great photo opportunities along the way; just don't dare stop in the mile-long tunnel. (RVers beware: there are size restrictions for vehicles in the tunnel.) The

Checkerboard Mesa that awaits you east of the tunnel is a visual experience completely different from the rest of the park. Enjoy, and be alert for many desert bighorn sheep here.

Once you reach the park's east entrance, turn around, and on your return trip stop to take the short hike up to **Canyon Overlook.** Once you descend again, you'll be ready to rest your feet at a screening of *Zion Canyon—Treasure of the Gods* at the **Zion Giant Screen Theater.** In the evening, you might want to attend a **ranger program** at one of the campground amphitheaters, or you can follow a relaxing dinner in **Springdale** with a stroll downtown.

ZION IN THREE DAYS

Take at least one signature hike, but slow down and don't attempt the Zion–Mt. Carmel Highway or push yourself to do the Riverside Walk on Day 1; however, do make a stop at the **visitor center** before it closes to help determine your plans for Day 2, especially if you plan an expedition that requires a permit.

Day 2 should start early, with a daybreak drive along the **Zion–Mt. Carmel Highway.** As the sun rises behind you, hike the short **Canyon Overlook** trail for stunning pictures of the south end of Zion Canyon. After returning through the tunnel, leave your car at **Canyon Junction** and take the shuttle all the way to **Temple of Sinawava**; you may want to pick up lunch or basic snacks at Zion Lodge on the way so you can stop for a picnic when the mood strikes. The **Riverside Walk** is a peaceful waterside wander for 1 mi, which deposits you at the mouth of the **Narrows.** This is Zion's most famous attraction. You don't need a permit or special training to wander up river, just heavy boots (or rent neoprene shoes in Springdale) and maybe a walking stick. Just wade in. Whether you follow the river around one bend or for 5 mi, it's a humbling experience where you're dwarfed by 2,000-foot cliffs above you.

Dry off and head back to you car and the town of Springdale. There are great restaurants, emerging galleries, and plenty of shops to enjoy. If you're lucky, catch live music at the outdoor amphitheater, a movie at the **Zion Giant Screen Theater,** or a dusk walk along the short **Watchman Trail** or **Pa'rus Trail**; if you're too exhausted to hike anymore, drop into an evening ranger talk.

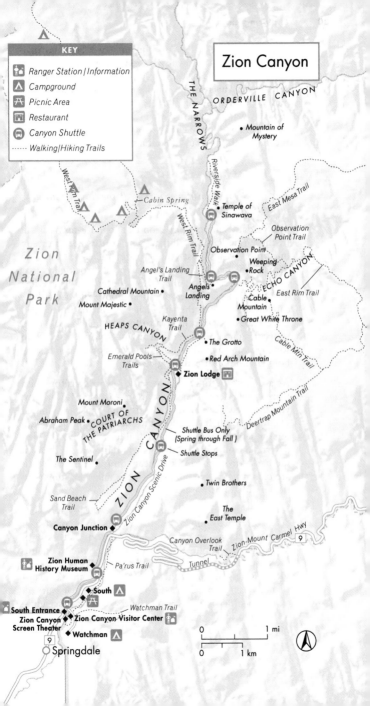

Zion Canyon

KEY

- Ranger Station / Information
- Campground
- Picnic Area
- Restaurant
- Canyon Shuttle
- Walking / Hiking Trails

ORDERVILLE CANYON

THE NARROWS

- Mountain of Mystery

Riverside Walk

East Mesa Trail

West Rim Trail

West 7th Trail

Cabin Spring

- Temple of Sinawava

Observation Point Trail

- Observation Point
- Weeping Rock

ECHO CANYON

Zion National Park

Angel's Landing Trail

- Angels Landing

East Rim Trail

- Cathedral Mountain
- Mount Majestic

- Cable Mountain

- Great White Throne

Kayenta Trail

HEAPS CANYON

- The Grotto

Cable Mtn Trail

Emerald Pools Trails

- Red Arch Mountain

◆ Zion Lodge

- Mount Moroni
- Abraham Peak
COURT OF THE PATRIARCHS

Deertrap Mountain Trail

- The Sentinel

Shuttle Bus Only (Spring through Fall)

Shuttle Stops

- Twin Brothers

ZION CANYON

- The East Temple

Sand Beach Trail

Zion Canyon Scenic Drive

Canyon Overlook Trail

Zion-Mount Carmel Hwy

9

Canyon Junction ◆

Tunnel

Zion Human History Museum

Pa'rus Trail

◆ **South**

Watchman Trail

South Entrance

Zion Canyon Screen Theater

◆ **Zion Canyon Visitor Center**

◆ **Watchman**

9

Springdale

0 ——— 1 mi

0 ——— 1 km

Explore an outlying area of Zion on Day 3. Head north to **Kolob Canyon**, where the **Taylor Creek Trail** follows the riverbed past two homesteaders' cabins to the memorable **Double Arch Alcove**. This relatively flat hike showcases water, rocks, and an ever-narrowing "finger" canyon. Summertime visitors may want to explore Cedar City from here, capping off a day with a Shakespearean play at the beautiful outdoor theater on the campus of Southern Utah University.

ZION CANYON

The park's main visitor center is at the South Entrance, just outside of Springdale.

The verdant sanctuary of Zion Canyon, a 6-mi oasis cut by the Virgin River, is all that some visitors need to see in one of the West's most-visited National Parks. There's no denying the beauty and scale of the solid rock cliffs that dwarf the stream-fed valley below. But with a little effort and a little more time, explorations above and beyond the canyon will unlock the vast riches of this national park. Landscapes range from lava to forest to slick rock, each supporting its unique ecosystem with wildlife from elk to songbirds and a rainbow-hue variety of flowers contrasting boldly with the surrounding desert.

As a driving destination, the park rewards visitors with three unique scenic passages. From I–15 near Cedar City, you can view the famous red cliffs and finger canyons. If you take Kolob Terrace Road to the center of the park, a remote series of trailheads are ideal for exploring the high desert plateau. But most drivers will relish the southern of the park—from the principal canyon (portions of which are closed to cars in summer) to the mile-long tunnel to the moonlike eastern portion of the park.

Similar to most national parks, however, the joy and wonder of Zion will only reveal themselves once you depart your vehicle. Short trails reward canyon visitors with incredible views, plus the sights and sounds of small animals and birds in their natural habitat. Feel the crisp, clear Virgin River carrying water that has taken thousands of years to seep through the surrounding stone. Measure 60 million geological years in the layers of rock descending down from the West Temple, 4,000 feet above you on the canyon floor. And if you find yourself here on a crisp summer night, take in one of the broadest spectrums of stars visible in North America.

VISITOR CENTERS

Zion Canyon National Park has two visitor centers, one for each section of the park, and they're both open year-round. The main center is at the south entrance of the park and is larger than the one at Kolob Canyon. There's a bookstore at each location, plus rangers to answer your questions or point you to a good hike or picnic area. Both feature exhibits and photographs that cover the park's natural and cultural history. Plan to get snacks, lunch, or coffee elsewhere.

Zion Canyon Visitor Center. Unlike most national park visitor centers, which are filled with indoor displays, Zion's presents most of its information in an appealing outdoor exhibit. Beneath shade trees beside a gurgling brook, displays help you plan your stay and introduce you to the area's geology, flora, and fauna. Inside, a large bookstore operated by the Zion Natural History Association sells field guides and other publications. **Ranger-guided shuttle tours** of Zion Canyon depart from the parking lot and travel to the Temple of Sinawava, with several photo-op stops along the way. The tour schedule and free tour tickets are available inside. You can also pick up backcountry permits here. ✉ *At south entrance, Zion Canyon* ☎ *435/772–3256* ⊕ *www.nps.gov/zion* ☉ *Apr. and May, daily 8–6; June–Oct., daily 8–8; Nov.–Mar., daily 8–5.*

SCENIC DRIVES

In the year 2000, National Park Service management decided to replace automobile access to the heart of Zion Canyon with 21 buses during high season. Rather than stifle this scenic drive, the move uncluttered traffic, emptied parking lots, reduced noise and emissions and has been well-received by millions of visitors. Cheerful, knowledgeable guides will make this "bus tour" an enjoyable, not just utilitarian ride.

With the exception of Zion Lodge, all of the park's services (and traffic) are clustered south of Canyon Junction. Keep this in mind as you ride the shuttle to the park's natural highlights, including the Court of the Patriarchs, Angel's Landing, Big Bend, and the Temple of Sinawava. There are six stops north of Canyon Junction, so if you only have

CLOSE UP

Good Reads

Here are a few useful volumes that will help you appreciate Zion National Park. All are available in the park's bookstores.

Towers of Stone, by J.L. Crawford, summarizes the essence of Zion National Park, its landscape, plants, animals, and human history.

Zion National Park: Sanctuary in the Desert, by Nicky Leach, gives you a photographic overview and a narrative journey through the park.

An Introduction to the Geology of Zion, by Al Warneke, contains information about the geology of Zion in a small booklet.

The Zion Tunnel, From Slickrock to Switchback, by Donald T. Garate, tells the fascinating story of the construction of the mile-long Zion Tunnel in the 1920s.

Wildflowers of Zion National Park, by Dr. Stanley L. Welsh, is always helpful during wildflower season.

one trip through this portion of the park, allow time to make multiple stops (buses run about every 7 minutes) to stretch your legs and get a better perspective on the towering formations above you.

Cars are still the primary way to see the park from November to March—and to drive the breath-taking Zion–Mt. Carmel Highway (regardless of time of year). Notably, the mile-long tunnel has size restrictions and escort requirements for RVs—so check the park Web site prior to your arrival or your vehicle may be turned around.

Zion Canyon Scenic Drive. Sheer, vividly colored cliffs tower 2,000 feet above the road that meanders along the floor of Zion Canyon. In high season, you can ride the park shuttle, which is a blessing. Guides will often point out wildlife, remnants of the 1994 "Sentinel" rockslide that dammed the Virgin River and forced evacuation of Zion Lodge and share historical and geological history about the park. As you roll through the narrow, steep canyon you'll pass the Court of the Patriarchs, the Sentinel, and the Great White Throne, among other imposing rock formations. Zion Canyon Scenic Drive is accessed only by park shuttle April through October, but you can drive it yourself the rest of the year. ⊠ *Zion Canyon.*

Zion–Mt. Carmel Highway. Two narrow tunnels lie between the east park entrance and Zion Canyon on this breath-taking 24-mi stretch of Route 9. As you travel through

The Shuttle System

Integrated with the gateway community of Springdale, quiet, propane-powered buses now serve the most visited portions of the park from March to October. Visitors staying in Springdale may leave their cars at their lodging and get anywhere in the park in minutes. If you're not staying in Springdale, look for six shuttle stops and Shuttle Parking signs where you can leave your vehicle while you explore the park.

Park officials are proud that the propane buses emit 98% fewer pollutants compared to gasoline-powered vehicles. Plus, the cost of propane is lower than gasoline and 85% of propane used in the United States is produced here.

In the heart of summer (May to September), the first bus departs the visitor center at 5:45 AM, with the last departure from Temple of Sinawava hitting the road at 11 PM. In March, April, and October, the first bus is at 6:45 AM and the last return departs the Temple of Sinawava at 10 PM. Schedules are subject to change, so check with a ranger or the latest edition of the Zion Map & Guide.

The nine buses that operate in the town of Springdale operate on roughly the same schedule as inside the park. Catch buses at (from south) Majestic View Lodge, Driftwood, Bit & Spur, Bumbleberry's, Flanigan's, and the Zion Canyon Theater.

solid rock from one end of the longest (1.1 mi) tunnel to the other, portals along one side provide a few glimpses of cliffs and canyons, and when you emerge on the other side you find that the landscape has changed dramatically. The tunnels are so narrow that large vehicles more than 7 feet, 10 inches wide or 11 feet, 4 inches high require traffic control while passing through; escorts are available 8 to 8 daily, April–October, and vehicles that use them must pay a $15 escort fee. ⊠ *Zion–Mt. Carmel Rte. 9, about 5 mi east of Canyon Junction, Zion Canyon.*

HISTORIC SITES

Zion Human History Museum. Enrich your visit with a stop here, where you can get a complete overview of the park with special attention to human history. Exhibits explain how settlers interacted with the geology, wildlife, plants, and unpredictable weather in the canyon from prehistory to the present. A 22-minute film, "Faces of Zion," plays throughout the day, revealing how natural forces shaped the park as we know it today. Learn about volcanic activity along the park's western boundary, the brief burst of energy that raised the Colorado plateau 10,000 feet in just a few million years and the role of water in the shaping the park. ⊠ *Zion Canyon Scenic Dr., 1 mi north of south entrance, Zion Canyon* ☎ *435/772-3256* ⊕ *www.nps.gov/zion/ HHMuseum.htm* ▢ *Free* ☉ *Late May–early Sept., daily 8–7; Sept. and mid-Apr.–late May, daily 8–6; Oct.–mid-Apr., daily 9–5.*

Zion Lodge. The Union Pacific Railroad constructed the first Zion National Park Lodge in 1925, with buildings designed by architect Stanley Gilbert Underwood. A fire destroyed the original building, but it was rebuilt to recapture some of the look and feel of the first building. The original Western-style cabins are still in use today. Among giant cottonwoods across the road from the Emerald Pools trailhead, the lodge houses a restaurant, snack bar, and gift shop. ⊠ *Zion Canyon Scenic Dr., about 3 mi north of Canyon JunctionZion Canyon* ☎ *435/772-7700* ⊕ *www. zionlodge.com.*

SCENIC STOPS

Checkerboard Mesa. The distinctive pattern on this huge, white mound of sandstone was created by a combination of vertical fractures and the exposure of horizontal bedding planes by erosion. This area is home to hundreds of bighorn sheep, which you may spot in large packs on the slopes—or sometimes grazing roadside. ⊠ *Zion–Mt. Carmel Hwy., 1 mi west of the east entrance, Zion Canyon.*

Court of the Patriarchs. This trio of peaks bears the names of, from left to right, Abraham, Isaac, and Jacob. Mount Moroni is the reddish peak on the far right, which partially blocks your view of Jacob. You can see the Patriarchs better by hiking a half-mile up Sand Bench Trail. Settler Isaac Behunin, who is credited with many of the religiously inspired names in the park, said "you can worship here as well as any manmade temple." ⊠*Zion Canyon Scenic Dr., 1½ mi north of Canyon Junction, Zion Canyon.*

Crawford Arch. From the north end of the parking lot at the Zion Human History Museum, look for a display pointing out an arch high on the western slope of the opposing hill. Crawford Arch is just to the right of a saddle slope in the ridge—and an easy one if you're keeping a "collection" of arches seen or visited in Utah. ⊠*Zion Canyon Scenic Dr., about 1 mi north of park entrance, Zion Canyon.*

Great White Throne. Towering over the Grotto picnic area near Zion Lodge is this massive 6,744-foot rock peak. ⊠*Zion Canyon Scenic Dr., about 3 mi north of Canyon Junction, Zion Canyon.*

Weeping Rock. A short, paved walk leads up to this flowing rock face, where wildflowers and delicate ferns thrive near a spring-fed waterfall that seeps out of a cliff. In fall, this area bursts with color. The 0.2-mi trail to the west alcove takes about 25 minutes round-trip. It is paved but too steep for wheelchairs. ⊠*Zion Canyon Scenic Dr., about 4 mi north of Canyon Junction, Zion Canyon.*

KOLOB CANYONS & KOLOB TERRACE

Often overlooked by park visitors, Kolob Canyons and Kolob Terrace offer a window into an entirely different habitat than that of Zion Canyon. About an hour from Springdale, the Kolob Canyons section gives you a peak into the red rock northwest corner of the park. Accessible from I–15 at Exit 40, nothing in the appearance of the unassuming visitor center hints at the lush red canyons that cut into the mountains behind it. The entire 5-mi road is within park boundaries with two trailheads offering day hikes, and one trailhead leading you into the vast backcountry of the park.

About 13 mi west of Springdale, Kolob Terrace Road takes visitors to lava fields, a reservoir, and a free (yes, free!) campground in the heart of the park's backcountry. Unlike Kolob Canyons Road, much of this road is outside of park boundaries, hopscotching through Bureau of Land Management and private land. Look for evidence of prehistoric volcanic activity in this region, with black rock prevailing here rather than the red clay and white sandstone that characterizes much of the rest of the park. There are several noteworthy peaks to see, several trailheads through which to access the backcountry, and, finally, Kolob Reservoir—a victim of too many dry years recently.

Kolob Canyons Area

KEY

👫	Ranger Station
△	Campground
🌲	Picnic Area
🍴	Restaurant
🏨	Lodge
⤳	Lookout

VISITOR CENTERS

This section of the park has a small visitor center with a bookstore, and rangers are on hand to answer your questions or point you to a good hike or picnic area. There's a small exhibit of photographs that cover the park's natural and cultural history. Plan to get snacks, lunch, or coffee elsewhere.

Kolob Canyons Visitor Center. This unassuming building is visible from I–15 and just yards away from the off-ramp at Exit 40, yet millions of drivers from Las Vegas to Salt Lake City skip it monthly. It will be their loss, not yours. Kolob Canyons Road disappears into the mountains less than a mile from the visitor center and unlocks a world of vivid red cliffs and "finger" canyons (so named for their resemblance to a hand as they cut into the western edge of the Colorado plateau). The center itself is basic (a ranger, some books and maps, and restrooms), but you can pick up backcountry permits here, saving you long lines in summer at the park's other visitor center. At the northwest entrance to Zion National Park, at I–15, Exit 40, just south of Cedar City. ✉ *At Kolob Canyons Entrance, Kolob Canyons* 🏨

Festivals & Events

St. George Winter Bird Festival. Numerous free bird-watching field trips, with destinations such as the Virgin River and Springdale vicinity are the highlight of this three-day festival each January. The Saturday evening banquet costs $20. ☎435/627–4560 ⊕www.redcliffsaudubon.org.

Hurricane Easter Car Show. Classic cars from all over the West descend on Hurricane for this event, which features a Friday dinner and Saturday's show each Easter weekend. An institution for more than 20 years, the show attracts about 7,000 people each year. On Easter Sunday there's a slow Rod Run through Zion National Park. ☎435/635–5720.

Western Legends Roundup. This nostalgic festival is for anyone with a love of cowboys, pioneer life, or Native American culture. For three days in August, the small town of Kanab fills with cowboy poets and storytellers, musicians, Western arts-and-crafts vendors, and Native American dancers and weavers. Wagon making, quilt shows, and a parade are all part of the fun. ☎435/644–3444 ⊕www.westernlegendsroundup.com.

Dixie Roundup. Sponsored by the St. George Lions Club, the Dixie Roundup rodeo has been a September tradition for decades. The real novelty of the professional event is that it's held on the green grass of Sun Bowl stadium. ☎435/628–8282.

St. George Marathon. With more than 10,000 applicants annually, this October marathon is one of the 20 biggest in the nation. Registration begins in April and the race turns people away annually. ☎435/627–4500.

435/772–3256 ⊕ *www.nps.gov/zion* ⊙ *Apr.–Oct., daily 8–5; Nov.–Mar., daily 8–4:30.*

SCENIC DRIVES

Hundreds of miles of scenic desert crisscross the Southwest, and Kolob Terrace Road will remind you of many of them. Sprawling as much as 4,000 feet above the floor of Zion Canyon, and without the benefit of the canyon's breezes and shade, the landscape is arid—browns and grays and ambers—but not without rugged beauty. Peaks and knolls emerge from the high plateau, birds circle overhead, and you might not see more than a half-dozen cars along this 22-mi stretch of road. The rewards are great, however, if you soak in the views from the trailheads near Lava Point or follow the "Subway" trail to the cliff's edge (about a mile from the trailhead).

Kolob Canyons, in contrast, is a 5-mi immersion in red rock canyons extending east-to-west along three forks of Taylor Creek and La Verkin Creek. At the end of the drive, take the short hike to the Kolob Canyons Viewpoint to see the Nagunt Mesa, Shuntavi Butte, and Gregory Butte, each rising to nearly 8,000 feet above sea level.

Kolob Canyons Road. From I–15 you get no hint of the beauty that awaits you on this 5-mi road. Most visitors gasp audibly when they get their first glimpse of the red canyon walls that rise suddenly and spectacularly out of the earth. The scenic drive winds amid these towers as it rises in elevation, until you reach a viewpoint that overlooks the whole Kolob region of Zion National Park. The shortest hike in this section of the park is the Kolob Canyons Viewpoint, an easy 30-minute walk in order to see a 360-degree panoramic view of this section of the park. Many hikers take the Middle Fork of Taylor Creek Trail, which is 2.7 mi one-way to Double Arch Alcove, along a peaceful riverbed. (*See Hiking, Sports & the Outdoors.*) During heavy snowfall Kolob Canyons Road may be closed. ⊠ *Kolob Canyons Rd. east of I–15, Exit 40, Kolob Canyons*

Kolob Terrace Road. A 44-mi round-trip drive takes you from Route 9 in Virgin to Lava Point for another perspective on the park. The winding drive overlooks the cliffs of the Left and Right forks of North Creek. From the road, if you're experienced in canyon hiking and canyoneering you can access a well-traveled but rough route up the Left Fork of North Creek, which leads all the way to the Subway, a stretch of the stream where the walls of the slot canyon close in so tightly as to form a near tunnel. Farther along the road, you reach the Northgate Peaks trailhead, where a path leads to a panorama of the Lower Kolob Plateau's crumpled and multihued topography. After passing near Lava Point, the road ends at the shallow waters of Kolob Reservoir outside park boundaries. ⊠*Starting from 13 mi west of Springdale in Virgin, Kolob Canyons*

SCENIC STOPS

Lava Point. At 7,890 feet above sea level, this spartan campground and picnic area is almost guaranteed to have different weather from Springdale. Catch your breath as you look far to the south across the top layer of the park. On frequent clear days, you can see the highest peaks of Zion and the gashes in the earth where the Virgin River and other creeks have carved canyons for millions of years. Look for extremely rare California condors on cliffs and cliffside trees in this area. The last mile to Lava Point is a scarcely maintained dirt road—use caution, and avoid the road entirely after heavy rains. ⊠*Kolob Terrace Rd., 20 mi north of Rte. 9, Kolob Canyons.*

Lee Pass. The hairpin turn on Kolob Canyons Road offers you a roadside pullout and an opportunity to glimpse deep into the canyon carved by the South fork of Taylor Creek. This is the trailhead for the Kolob Arch hike, which also connects you to the main section of Zion National Park via the backcountry. Don't head to the wilderness without a backcountry permit. ⊠*Kolob Canyons Rd., 3 mi southwest of Kolob Canyons Entrance, Kolob Canyons.*

North Creek Left Fork Trail. The trailhead for hikers wishing to hike to the Subway "from the bottom up," this parking area is adjacent to sharp, black lava fields interspersed with hearty cacti. Follow the trail about 1 mi to the cliff's edge, where Subway hikers descend to the river and head upstream to the Subway. Watch birds circle in front of the cliff face to the north. Don't head down the steep trail without a permit from park rangers. ⊠*Kolob Terrace Rd., 7 mi north of Rt. 9, Kolob Canyons.*

Timber Creek Overlook. At the end of Kolob Canyons Road, pause for a picnic and stare down the tips of the "finger" canyons to the east. Shuntavi Butte juts out from Timber Top Mountain (8,075 feet) to the southeast of you. Follow the contours of Timber Creek to see where intrepid hikers go to see what is possibly the country's largest freestanding natural arch—Kolob Arch. It's a 14-mi round-trip by foot, however, so don't get any ideas without first consulting the backcountry ranger at the visitor center. ⊠*Kolob Canyons Rd., 5 mi southwest of Kolob Canyons Entrance, Kolob Canyons.*

Zion Hikes &
Other Activities

WORD OF MOUTH

"Angels Landing and The Narrows are two of the top hikes to be done in America. You can look on a lot of top 10 hikes, and these two appear very often."

—spirobulldog

By Steve
Pastorino

**ZION CANYON OFFERS VISITORS PLENTY OF OPPORTU-
NITIES** to get out of the car for recreation, with activities
suited to all ages and abilities. Hiking is by far the most
popular activity in the park, ranging from 30-minute level
walks in the canyon to 3-day backcountry canyoneering
excursions to the famous Narrows and Subway. Some of
the most popular hikes, including Angel's Landing, involve
substantial elevation gain, so be aware of your physical
abilities and limits.

Cyclists rejoiced when Zion Canyon was deemed off limits
to cars during the busy summer season. Bicycles are not
allowed in the tunnel, but that doesn't stop some from
climbing the Zion–Mt. Carmel Highway, so look out for
them on any park road. You may bring your bicycle on the
shuttles (space permitting), so a one-way ride from your
hotel to Temple of Sinawava is a fun way to see the park.
It's also possible to explore on horseback. Take a day trip
with Canyon Trail Rides, or bring your own horses on
some backcountry trails.

Ranger-led activities include hikes, twice-daily shuttle tours,
lodge talks, campground programs, and full moon walks
in the summer. Kids can become junior rangers: bone up in
advance online at ⊕ *www.nps.gov/zion* if you like.

In the surrounding area, world-class mountain biking and
road cycling is possible. Additionally, several outfitters can
arrange canyoneering, climbing, riding, and family hiking
trips, but commercial guides are not allowed to operate
inside the park. In winter, hiking boots can be exchanged
for snowshoes and cross-country skis, but check with a
ranger to determine backcountry snow conditions.

DAY HIKES

The best way to experience Zion Canyon is to walk beneath,
between, and, if you can bear it (and have good balance!),
along its towering cliffs. There's something for everyone,
from paved and flat river strolls to precarious cliff-side
scrambles.

Zion rangers suggest 14 frontcountry hikes, none of which
requires a permit. Eleven of these hikes can be accessed
directly from the Zion Canyon Scenic Drive; three are in the
Kolob Canyons section of the park. You can buy detailed
guides and maps to the trails of Zion National Park at the
Zion Canyon Visitor Center bookstore.

BEST BETS FOR ACTIVITIES

■ **Soar to Angel's Landing:** Climb nearly 1,500 feet, and tread lightly along narrow passages, to peer out from Zion Canyon's most awe-inspiring and best-known viewpoints.

■ **Find your personal sanctuary:** Native Americans have known about Zion Canyon for 1,000 years. The steep walls, canyon breezes, and lush flora still offer peace for those who seek it.

■ **Stone-stepping up the narrows:** The crystal, chilly waters of the Virgin River are so tempting you'll want to walk to at least the first bend

. . . then the next . . . then the next. Start at Temple of Sinawava for a true "river walk."

■ **Zion–Mt. Carmel Highway:** The switchbacks to the east of Canyon Junction are just the prelude for the crescendo, a 1.2-mi long tunnel and the finale, the moonscape of Checkerboard Mesa.

■ **You can't get up there from down here:** The Narrows and Subway are legendary treks that require a backcountry permit to enter from the top, but each is more accessible from the bottom than you might think.

One conspicuous absence on the list of 14 hikes is the Narrows, which has a false reputation as accessible only via a two-day backcountry hike. On a dry, clear day, one look at the Virgin River at the end of the Riverside Walk will demonstrate what many people figure out quite easily on their own; anyone can wade into the river upstream toward the Narrows; even better, no permit is required to travel the first 5 mi. Good hiking or wading boots are a must, and a walking stick is optional. You won't get far barefoot, and the slippery rocks can be too much for sandals. But you don't need to buy this gear; you can rent everything you need in Springdale. Past the first bend, you may spend as little as 50% of the time in the water (ranging from ankle-deep to waist-deep) as there are sand bars, small beaches, and short trails along the way. Be sure to ask a ranger about the potential for flash floods.

There are more than a dozen backcountry trails in the park, including an epic walk from Kolob Canyons to Zion Canyon following La Verkin Creek, Hop Valley, Wildcat Canyon, and the West Rim (allow three to five days for this trek).

Whether you're heading out for a day of rock hopping or an hour of strolling, you should carry—and drink—plenty of water to counteract the effects of southern Utah's arid climate. Wear a hat, sunscreen, and sturdy shoes or boots; make sure to bring a map, and be honest with yourself about your capabilities. Getting in over your head can have serious health consequences.

HIKES TO LOOK OUT FOR
Hikes are listed in our order of preference.

Short hikes (less than two hours): Riverside Walk, Weeping Rock, Emerald Pools Trail, Canyon Overlook Trail, Grotto Trail, Pa'Rus Trail, Watchman Trail, Timber Creek Overlook.

Half-day hikes (up to five hours): Angel's Landing, Observation Point, Taylor Creek Trail, Hidden Canyon.

Full-day hikes: Narrows Trail (from the bottom up), the Subway, Kolob Arch.

ZION CANYON

SPOTLIGHT HIKE: THE NARROWS FROM TEMPLE OF SINAWAVA
On a sizzling summer day, no walk is more refreshing or tantalizing than a mile or two *in* the Virgin River starting at Temple of Sinawava. No permit is required to wander as far as 5 mi upstream, but flash floods are a real hazard, so check with a ranger before you go. (Ask about conditions to visit the Narrows "from the bottom up.") Even outdoor novices and kids can handle the first few hundred yards without special preparation—allow an hour. More experienced and physically fit hikers will love the 10-mi round-trip—allow at least five hours. ⊠ *End of Zion Canyon Rd., at Temple of Sinawava, Zion Canyon* ⚐ *Difficult.*

0.0 MI: TEMPLE OF SINAWAVA
From the Temple of Sinawava shuttle stop, follow the 1-mi Riverside Walk until it ends. In warm, dry weather, you may find dozens of people wading ankle-deep upstream. Even without special gear, most people can make it to the first bend. Watch your footing on the smooth and slippery rocks ("like walking on slick bowling balls"), but also look up and marvel at 1,000-foot canyon walls above you.

THE NARROWS TRAIL TIPS

■ The one-of-a-kind beauty of the Narrows can be deadly. Late summer brings monsoon rains to Zion, which can trigger flash floods. Canyon floods quickly overwhelm everything in their path with debris-filled water sometimes dozens of feet deep. Flash floods are rare, but don't enter the Narrows without explicit permission from a ranger.

■ Flip-flops don't cut it. Water-resistant sandals (like Tevas) take a beating as well. Wear sturdy waterproof boots, or rent neoprene river shoes from Zion Adventure Company or another outfitter in town.

■ Even the most balanced of hikers can slip on the rocks, crevices, or fast-flowing water that test your every step. If you're going to bring an expensive camera, phone, glasses, or other valuable items, carry them in a waterproof case high on your body (around your neck or shoulders, not your waist).

■ Have fun. The Zion Narrows can be intimidating—and the top-down approach should be left to advanced hikers. But a walk up the river from Temple of Sinawava is a once-in-a-lifetime experience that is hard to replicate anywhere in the world.

1.5 MI: MYSTERY CANYON FALLS

The first half-mile in the river might take 30 minutes or more. After one or two bends, you may quickly find yourself facing 2- to 3-foot deep water. It's time to decide how far you want to go. Take heart, for much of this hike, the deeper stretches last only a few yards, then you're rock hopping again. After a half-mile in the water, look and listen for the cascading waterfall on the canyon's east side.

2.5 MI: ORDERVILLE CANYON

Zion Canyon splits to reveal a canyon often fed by not much more than an inch or two of water. Orderville Canyon is tantalizing, but you won't get far before you realize that deep pools and tall waterfalls impair your upstream explorations. Look for hikers coming downstream; they've hiked a dozen miles, rappelled, swam, and possibly even camped overnight to get to this point.

3.5 MI: WALL STREET

This is why you came. The canyon narrows to as little as 22 feet, and with 1,500-foot cliffs above, you are truly humbled by the sculpting power of the river. For about

2 mi, lurch from dry shoreline to tiny sand beaches; clamber over rocks and feel the chill of the water, which is sometimes as much as waist deep.

5.0 MI: BIG SPRINGS

Congratulations, you outlasted the throngs. Find a dry perch on the landing opposite the Big Springs boulder, which juts into the river with a steady stream of water nourishing the mosses that cover it. Traveling any farther upstream requires a permit, but don't bother—it becomes more and more difficult without ropes and guides. Enjoy your accomplishment, then plunge back in—the only way out is the way you came in.

SPOTLIGHT HIKE: ANGEL'S LANDING

The park's signature hike, this strenuous ascent from the floor of Zion Canyon rewards your effort with utterly immaculate views. Persevere through a series of switchbacks known as "Walter's Wiggles," and you can find yourself at Scout Lookout, a perfectly stunning (but false) summit. But wait, there's more. If you don't fear heights, Angel's Landing is only a few hundred yards away. Allow four hours for this 5-mi round-trip. ⊠ *Zion Canyon Scenic Dr., about 4½ mi north of Canyon Junction, Zion Canyon* ↝ *Difficult.*

0.0 MI: THE GROTTO

Ride the shuttle to the Grotto, then cross the river and follow the signs. Walk parallel to the Virgin River for ½ mi, looking for wildlife on the shoreline especially near dawn and dusk. You gradually begin to climb when you see the first series of switchbacks luring you ever steeper and higher.

1.0 MI: REFRIGERATOR CANYON

This hanging canyon is carved between soaring walls on either side of you. Note the geological map that climbs hundreds of feet on either side of you—red clays and pink-and-white granite, with vegetation stubbornly clinging to the walls. As you approach Walter's Wiggles, bear in mind that this trail was built in the 1920s without the use of modern-day tools.

1.6 MI: WALTER'S WIGGLES

Twenty-one switchbacks are steep but not narrow or vertigo-inducing. Imagine what it took park superintendent

ANGEL'S LANDING TRAIL TIPS

■ The elevation change is 1,500 feet over 2.5 mi, meaning lots of switchbacks, stair-climbing, and plain old trudging. This trail is not for the faint of heart, so know your limits and go slow.

■ As for most any Zion excursion, prepare for intense sun year-round and/or extreme weather changes. This is not an ordinary 5-mi hike, so bring water, a snack, or lunch, and allow plenty of time to ascend and descend. The way down, by the way, might take you as little as half as long as your climb.

■ To avoid crowds, go early ... really early. This is a popular trail in a popular park, so don't come to Angel's Landing expecting to have it to yourself.

■ For an equally strenuous hike with a rewarding view and a fraction of the company, try Observation Point instead.

3

Walter Ruesch to carve this path into the solid rock in 1926, as you steadily put one foot in front of the other.

1.9 MI: SCOUT LOOKOUT

The destination for many hikers, Scout Lookout rises 1,000 feet above the valley floor. It's a perfect spot for a photograph, a snack, or lunch break, or to hook onto the West Rim Trail and head into Zion's backcountry. If you're okay with heights and narrow passages, however, grab the railings and wander across the narrow neck to the Angel's Landing peninsula.

2.5 MI: ANGEL'S LANDING

You can see Angel's Landing from several spots along the hike, but it's not until you walk across a 3- to 5-foot "bridge" from Scout Lookout that you see how challenging it is to reach the 5,790-foot perch. You have to wonder how the National Park Service risk-management people still allow people to clamber up the steep rocks, where one slip can mean a perilous fall. In the end, step out onto a white granite tabletop and peer out for miles in every direction.

OTHER TRAILS

★ Fodor'sChoice **Canyon Overlook Trail.** If your health or fear of ☾ heights keeps you from the popular Angel's Landing, try this short walk for a stunning view with a fraction of the work. Find the trailhead immediately east of the Zion–Mt. Carmel tunnel. The trail is moderately steep but only

1 mi round-trip; allow an hour to hike it. The overlook at trail's end gives you views of the West and East Temples, Towers of the Virgin, the Streaked Wall, and other Zion Canyon cliffs and peaks. You can also marvel at the tunnel's engineering. ⊠ *Rte. 9, east of Zion–Mt. Carmel Tunnel, Zion Canyon* ☞ *Easy.*

☾ **Emerald Pools Trail.** Two small waterfalls cascade (or drip, in dry weather) into pools named for the algae that sometimes make the water shimmer. The way is paved up to the lower pool and is suitable for baby strollers and wheelchairs with assistance. Beyond the lower pool, the trail becomes rocky and steep as you progress toward the middle and upper pools. Don't pass up the Upper Pool; it's hands-down the most stunning and only a few hundred more yards. After the Middle pool, the trail cuts in and around massive boulders jutting out into the path. Upper Pool features a clear lagoon at the base of a vegetation-rich cliff and a 300-foot waterfall. This is a great spot for a photograph and/or a picnic, but remember, no swimming allowed. On your descent, negotiate a crevice not more than 2 feet wide to connect with the Grotto Trail. A less crowded and exceptionally enjoyable return route follows the Kayenta Trail an additional mile or so to the north before reconnecting with the Grotto Trail. Allow 50 minutes round-trip to the lower pool and 2½ hours round-trip to the middle and upper pools. ⊠ *Zion Canyon Scenic Dr., about 3 mi north of Canyon Junction, Zion Canyon* ☞ *Easy–moderate.*

☾ **Grotto Trail.** This flat and easy trail takes you from Zion Lodge to the Grotto picnic area, traveling for the most part along the park road. Allow 20 minutes or less for the walk. If you're up for a longer hike—and have two to three hours—connect with the Kayenta Trail after you cross the footbridge and head for the Emerald Pools. You will begin gaining elevation, and it's a steady climb to the pools. ⊠ *Zion Canyon Scenic Dr., about 3 mi north of Canyon Junction, Zion Canyon* ☞ *Easy.*

Hidden Canyon Trail. This steep, 2-mi round-trip hike takes you up 850 feet in elevation. Not too crowded, the trail is paved all the way to Hidden Canyon. Allow about three hours for the round-trip hike. ⊠ *Zion Canyon Scenic Dr., 3¼ mi north of Canyon Junction, Zion Canyon* ☞ *Moderate.*

Observation Point. More than one park ranger says this is their favorite hike. Three miles longer than Angel's Landing and with 50% more vertical elevation gain, this strenuous hike is too much for many—meaning you'll have much more solitude. The 8-mi, half-day (five-hour) round-trip trek takes you past rocks bursting with moisture between towering cliffs and rewards you with a view down into Big Bend and Zion Canyon. You can even look *down* on Angel's Landing. ⊠ *Zion Canyon Scenic Dr., 4 mi north of Canyon Junction, Zion Canyon* ☞ *Difficult.*

Pa'rus Trail. This 2-mi walking and biking path parallels and occasionally crosses the Virgin River, starting at South Campground and proceeding north along the river to the beginning of Zion Canyon Scenic Drive. It's paved and gives you great views of the Watchman, the Sentinel, the East and West Temples, and Towers of the Virgin. Dogs are allowed on this trail as long as they are leashed. Cyclists must follow traffic rules on this heavily used trail. ⊠ *Canyon Junction, ½ mi north of south entrance, Zion Canyon* ☞ *Easy.*

Riverside Walk. Beginning at the Temple of Sinawava shuttle stop at the end of Zion Canyon Scenic Drive, this easily enjoyed 1-mi round-trip stroll shadows the Virgin River. The river gurgles by on one side of the trail; on the other, wildflowers bloom out of the canyon wall in fascinating hanging gardens. This is the park's most trekked trail; it's paved and suitable for baby strollers and for wheelchairs with assistance. A round-trip walk takes between one and two hours. The end of the trail marks the beginning of the Narrows Trail. ⊠ *Zion Canyon Scenic Dr., 5 mi north of Canyon Junction, Zion Canyon* ☞ *Easy.*

Watchman Trail. For a view of the town of Springdale and a look at lower Zion Creek Canyon and the Towers of the Virgin, take the moderately strenuous hike that begins on a service road east of Watchman Campground. Some springs seep out of the sandstone to nourish hanging gardens and attract wildlife here. There are a few sheer cliff edges on this route, so children should be supervised carefully. Allow two hours for this 3-mi hike. ⊠ *East of Rte. 9 (main park road), on access road inside south entrance, Zion Canyon* ☞ *Moderate.*

Weeping Rock. A half-mile round-trip, this is definitely a kid-friendly trail. Hop off the bus three stops from the north end of the park. The well-marked trail is shaded and has a steady incline that leads to steps as you approach the alcove. Although much of the trail is paved, the steepness and irregularity may make it difficult for strollers and wheelchairs. Amaze your kids when you tell them the water trickling down on them has taken more than 1,000 years to seep down and through Echo Canyon. ⊠ *Zion Canyon Scenic Dr., 4 mi north of Canyon Junction, Zion Canyon* ☞ *Easy.*

KOLOB CANYONS

SPOTLIGHT HIKE: TAYLOR CREEK TRAIL

The principal day-hike in the Kolob Canyons section of the park, this 6-mi hike offers a grand payoff: the Double Arch Alcove. Enjoy a peaceful walk along the Middle fork of Taylor Creek beneath ever narrower, impossibly high canyon walls, before you round a corner to the pair of arches. ⊠ *Kolob Canyons Rd., about 1½ east of Kolob Canyons Visitor Center, Kolob Canyons* ☞ *Moderate.*

0.0 MI: TRAILHEAD

Enter the Kolob Canyon section of the park from Exit 40 off I–15. The trailhead is about 1.5 mi up Kolob Canyons Road on the north side. A short, steep descent takes you to the creek bed, where trees provide cover and breezes help mitigate the summer sun. Head upstream, choosing between a well-marked path and rock-hopping in the cool, clear water.

0.5 MI: PHOTO OP

You can't miss the giant boulder that blocks the right side of the trail. Improbably it has a twisted cottonwood tree seemingly growing out of the top of it. You'll pass "under" a huge rock later.

1.5 MI / 2.0 MI: CABINS FEVER

Larson and Fife cabins pop up within a half-mile of one another. Built by 19th-century homesteaders, each is about 10 feet by 15 feet with stout timber sides, a couple of window openings, and an old door. You can't enter either, but you can certainly imagine the hardy souls who trekked up the same creek bed to establish their homes more than 100 years ago.

2.7 MI: DOUBLE ARCH ALCOVE

Neither arch here is of the freestanding variety (like Kolob Arch), but you'll feel like you've found two pots of gold at the end of a rainbow. The primary alcove is a giant grotto, 100 yards across, with moist vegetation growing up its base. (Please heed the signs imploring hikers not to tread

TAYLOR CREEK TRAIL TIPS

■ The entire Kolob Canyons section of the park receives about 10% of the visitors that Zion Canyon receives, so revel in the peace and tranquillity. On the other hand, you're in a remote canyon, so don't expect to get a signal on your cell phone if something goes wrong. Be prepared with water, food, and sturdy walking shoes.

■ For a flatter walk back to the trailhead, take the creek bed itself. You may have to brush aside some vegetation or clamber over a downed log or two, but the keen

eye will spot deer tracks, butterflies, lizards, and tiny, tumbling terraces of water. Beware of boulders, fallen trees, flashflood debris, not to mention the missing the exit sign, which sits at the base of two sets of wood "stairs" just below the parking lot. If you walk too far, you can hear cars from the Kolob Canyons entrance road overhead.

■ This is a day hike only. No camping is allowed in Taylor Creek Canyon. The nearest backcountry campsites in Kolob Canyon area are on La Verkin Creek Trail.

on this delicate microclimate.) A few steps later, you see a second arch carved into the side of the reddish cliff above. You can continue a few hundred yards farther in the creek bed, but soon debris blocks your way. Turn around—the only way out is the way you came.

OTHER TRAILS

Kolob Arch. In the park's northwest corner, a 7-mi one-way hike leads you to one of the largest freestanding arches ever discovered. Kolob Arch spans nearly the length of a football field (287 feet) and is reached via a pleasant trail alongside La Verkin Creek and beneath the vivid red cliffs of Shuntavi Butte and Timber Top Mountain (8,075 feet). Multiple campsites are available to make this an overnight itinerary (a permit is required for an overnight stay). Connect to the Hop Valley Trail to head into the main portion of Zion National Park. ⊠ *Lee Pass Trailhead is approx. 3 mi east of Kolob visitor center on Kolob Canyons Rd., Kolob Canyons* ⚐*Moderate.*

The Subway. The Left Fork of Middle Creek is one of the most awe-inspiring mapped features of Zion (the locals, though, are hiding some from outsiders). It requires a permit, even for a relatively moderate day hike, but determined hikers can easily manage its 11-mi round-trip trek from "the bottom up" if you can get a permit. (A limited number of permits are available on 24 hours' notice; arrive at the Zion Visitor Center by 7 AM if you hope to get one.) This journey begins with a mile-long hike across the black-lava field remnants of an ancient volcanic eruption. Then negotiate a steep descent to the riverbed and head upstream. Highlights include intersections with several smaller canyon streams and a 30-foot trailside slab of dinosaur prints (on the north side of the creek just past the second connecting canyon—ask a ranger at the Kolob Canyons Visitor Center to show you on a map). Mostly, though, you have the pristine serenity of the river carving slick rock and then the Subway itself. You may have to climb up a watery incline or two, as the river's width moistens the entire creek bed, but the Subway will be worth it. Think of a subway tunnel with a river of water emanating from it instead of a train— then enter at your own risk. ⊠ *Kolob Terrace Rd., about 7 mi north of Rte. 9, Kolob Canyons* ☞ *Difficult.*

☾ **Timber Creek Overlook.** Don't miss this short hike at the end of the Kolob Canyons Road. It's barely a mile round-trip on a sandy, relatively exposed plateau above the surrounding valleys. Get a good look at the Kolob Canyons "skyline," including Maugent Mountain and Shuntavi Butte, each in the shadow of 8,055-foot Timber Top Mountain. The last few hundred yards are a little rockier with a 100-foot ascent, but most children and senior citizens shouldn't have any problems with it. As with many locations in the park, this trailhead starts at more than a mile above sea level—6,250 feet. Also, the picnic area 100 yards from the trailhead offers four tables, ample shade, and a suitable spot for little ones to chase after lizards, chipmunks, squirrels, and the occasional long-eared, black tail jackrabbit. ⊠ *At end of Kolob Canyons Rd., about 5 mi from Kolob Canyons Visitor Center, Kolob Canyons* ☞ *Easy.*

SUMMER SPORTS & ACTIVITIES

ADVENTURE TOURS

Zion Adventure Company (⊠ *868 Zion Park Blvd., Springdale* ☎ *435/772–0990* ⊕ *www.zionadventures.com*) has guided, equipped, and offered advice on a menagerie of desert adventures since 1996. Countless tourists heading upstream on the Narrows carry Zion Adventure walking sticks and neoprene aqua sox footwear. The company also provides shuttle service to Zion's major canyoneering hikes (including the Narrows, Subway, Mystery Canyon, and Orderville Canyon) and offers guided backcountry explorations outside of the park (for adults, families, and kids as young as 5), wilderness training, stargazing, and more. The friendly staff will indulge every "silly" question in their quest to get you on the trail—and home again—safely.

Zion Rock Guides (⊠ *1458 Zion Park Blvd., Springdale* ☎ *435/ 772–3303* ⊕ *www.zionrockguides.com*) takes visitors (including families and children) on climbing, canyoneering, cycling, and jeep routes all over southern Utah's backcountry. (No outfitter can lead groups into Zion's legendary Narrows, Subway, or Orderville Canyon routes, although they can provide advice and equipment.) Friendly owner Dean Woods is one of the region's eminent authorities on climbing since the 1970s.

AIR TOURS

Bryce Canyon Airlines & Helicopters (☎ *435/834–5341* ⊕ *www. rubysinn.com/bryce-canyon-airlines.html* ✈ *$75*) offers a once-in-a-lifetime view of Zion National Park. Join professional pilots and guides for an airplane ride over the park (and Bryce Canyon National Park during the same flight). Flights depart from Ruby's Inn Heliport near the entrance to Bryce Canyon.

BICYCLING

The introduction of the park shuttle has improved bicycling conditions in Zion National Park, for during the busy months, April through October, cyclists no longer share Zion Canyon Scenic Drive with thousands of cars—though two-wheelers do need to be cautious of the large buses plying the park road throughout the day. Within the park proper, bicycles are only allowed on established park roads and on the 3½-mi Pa'rus Trail, which winds along the Virgin River in Zion Canyon. You cannot ride your bicycle through the Zion–Mt. Carmel tunnels; the only way to get your bike past this stretch of the highway is to transport it by motor vehicle.

Outside the park, southern Utah is home to a booming road cycling community. Ask at any bike shop in the region for favorite routes. Mountain bikers are increasingly drawn to Gooseberry Mesa, which locals consider equal or better than the famous Moab slick rock mountain biking trails.

Bicycles Unlimited (⊠*90 S. 100 E, St. George* ☎*888/673–4492* ⊕ *www.bicyclesunlimited.com*) has a treasure trove of information on mountain biking in southern Utah, they rent bikes and sell parts, accessories, and guidebooks.

Bike Zion (⊠*1458 Zion Park Blvd., Springdale* ☎ *435/772–3303* ⊕ *www.bikingzion.com*) rents Kona and Jamis bikes and sets up supported road cycling trips and single-track and/or slickrock adventures at nearby Gooseberry Mesa. The company also rents car racks and trailers and can give you tips on the local trails. Day trips and multiday tours are available. Ask them about the best area trails if you prefer to explore on your own.

Zion Cycles (⊠*868 Zion Park Blvd., Springdale* ☎ *435/772–0400* ⊕ *www.zioncycles.com*), a busy bicycle shop, is in the heart of Springdale in the same converted church complex where you can pick up pasta, artwork, and reading materials while waiting for our bike tune-up. Rent Trek mountain bikes, LeMond road bikes, pick up trail advice, and/or join one of their mountain or road tours throughout southern Utah.

ZION'S BIRDS. Approximately 290 bird species call Zion Canyon home or else pass through its environs on occasion. Some species, such as the white-throated swift and the powerful peregrine falcon, take full advantage of the towering cliffs. Closer to the ground are the common pinyon jay and, if you look closely enough, perhaps a Gambel's quail. Wild turkeys are not only common, but some aren't very wild, venturing up to visitors looking for a handout. If you're quick, you might spot one of nine species of hummingbirds that have been spotted feeding at various Zion Canyon blossoms.

ROCK CLIMBING

The climbing in southern Utah is considered world-class. Keep your eyes peeled on Zion's Scenic road for gear-laden climbers heading up intimidating vertical faces. Park officials recommend March through May and September through November as best times to climb inside the park. No permit is required.

Zion Rock Guides (⊠*1458 Zion Park Blvd., Springdale* ☎ *435/772–3303* ⊕ *www.zionrockguides.com*) offers climbing expeditions from beginner (including children ages 7+)

ROCK CLIMBING TIPS

■ Sandstone is weak when wet. Avoid climbing in damp areas or after rain.

■ Because of Zion's 2,000-foot cliffs, few areas are suitable for top roping.

■ Two prime bouldering opportunities exist within ½ mi of the south entrance—a ranger can direct you to either one.

■ Some rock formations may be closed from May through July due to peregrine falcon nesting. Some areas that are routinely closed include the Great White Throne, Cable Mountain, Court of the Patriarchs, and the Streaked Wall.

to expert. Rates start at $75 per day depending on group size and itinerary.

FISHING

The waterfalls and rough terrain of the Virgin River and its nearby creeks do not make for ideal fishing conditions. Still, fishing is allowed as long as you have a Utah State fishing license. You may catch (and keep) trout. Just outside the park, Kolob Reservoir (8,000 feet above sea level) offers decent but unspectacular trout angling. Look for the dirt road at the end of Kolob Terrace Road, about 5 mi north of Lava Point.

HORSEBACK RIDING

Grab your hat and boots and see Zion Canyon the way the pioneers did—on the back of a horse or mule. This is a sure way to make your trip to Zion National Park memorable. Only one outfitter is licensed to guide tours within park boundaries. Easygoing, one-hour and half-day trips are available, with a minimum age of 7 and 10 years respectively. Maximum weight on either trip is 220 pounds.

The friendly folks at **Canyon Trail Rides** (⊠*Zion Canyon Scenic Dr., across road from Zion Lodge, Zion Canyon* ☎ *435/679–8665* ⊕ *www.canyonrides.com* ⊠ *$30–$65*) have been around for years, and they are the only outfitter for trail rides inside the park. Departing from corrals across the grassy meadow from Zion Lodge, their one-hour and half-day rides allow you to see Zion in a truly Western way. Anyone over age 7 can participate. The horses work from late March through October; you may want to make reservations ahead of time.

SWIMMING

Swimming is allowed in the Virgin River within and outside park boundaries, but be careful of cold water, slippery rock bottoms, and the occasional flash flood whenever it rains. Swimming is not allowed in the Emerald Pools, and the use of inner tubes is prohibited within park boundaries.

WINTER SPORTS & ACTIVITIES

Cross-country skiing and snowshoeing are best experienced in the park's higher elevations in winter, where snow stays on the ground longer. Inquire at the Zion Canyon Visitor Center for backcountry conditions. Snowmobiling is only allowed for residential access.

EXPLORING THE BACKCOUNTRY

Zion offers a vast backcountry spanning elevations from less than 4,000 feet above sea level to as high as 8,000 feet. The wild lands encompass perilously deep canyons, forested plateaus, and broad slickrock mesas. Water is at a premium in this extreme climate, much of which can be considered unforgiving desert. Three trails are often included among the nation's favorites: Orderville Canyon, the Narrows, and the Subway, but there are other popular backcountry trails in the park.

GETTING A BACKCOUNTRY PERMIT IN ZION

At least 25% of all permits are held for walk-in visitors for same-day or next-day trips. Check at either visitor center (the main Zion Valley visitor center opens at 7 AM in summer; the center at Kolob Canyons opens at 8 AM) to apply for a permit. Backcountry fees are based on your group's size: $10 for 1 or 2 people; $15 for 3 to 7 people; $20 for 8 to 12 people.

The remaining permits are assigned in advance. From April through October, reservations are allocated via an online lottery three months in advance. For example, you must

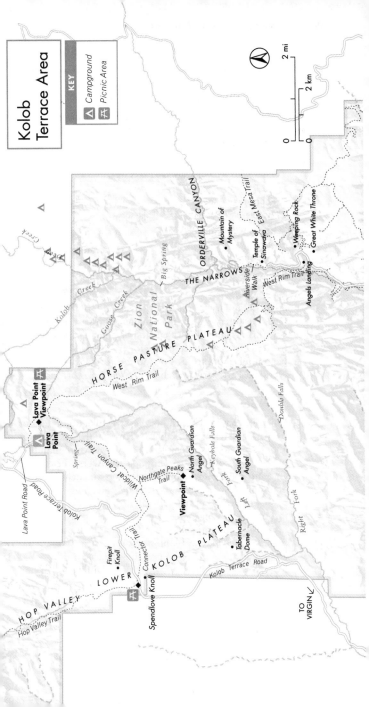

Kolob
Terrace Area

KEY

⛺ Campground
🍴 Picnic Area

2 mi
2 km

ZION NATIONAL PARK

Kolob Creek

Willis Creek

Goose Creek

Big Spring

THE NARROWS

ORDERVILLE CANYON

Mountain of Mystery

Temple of Sinawava

East Mesa Trail

Weeping Rock

Great White Throne

Riverside Walk

West Rim Trail

Angels Landing

HORSE PASTURE PLATEAU

West Rim Trail

Lava Point Viewpoint

Lava Point

Double Falls

Springs

Wildcat Canyon Trail

Northgate Peaks Trail

North Guardian Angel

South Guardian Angel

Keyhole Falls

Left Fork

Right Fork

Viewpoint

KOLOB PLATEAU

Tabernacle Dome

Kolob Terrace Road

TO VIRGIN

Firepit Knoll

Spendlove Knoll

Connector Trail

LOWER

HOP VALLEY

Hop Valley Trail

Lava Point Road

Kolob Terrace Road

2008 Backcountry Use Limits

CLOSE UP

Each major area in the Zion backcountry has its own limits. Here are the limits for 2008 to use as a reference.

■ **Behunin Canyon,** 12 people/day

■ **Echo Canyon,** 12 people/day

■ **Englestead Canyon,** 12 people/day

■ **Keyhole Canyon,** 80 people/day

■ **La Verkin Creek,** 17 groups/night

■ **Mystery Canyon,** 12 people/day

■ **Orderville Canyon,** 50 people/day

■ **Pine Creek Canyon,** 50 people/day

■ **Spry Canyon,** 12 people/day

■ **Subway (Left Fork),** 80 people/day

■ **West Rim,** 9 groups/night

■ **Zion Narrows,** 12 groups/night & 40 day users

apply in January for the lottery that hands out April dates. Once the lottery is held, any remaining spots are made available through an online calendar. For example, reservations for April trips not filled by the lottery are available online beginning February 5. For more information, visit the National Park Service Web site (⊕ *www.nps.org/zion*).

RECOMMENDED TRAILS

Orderville Canyon. This 12-mi, one-way hike begins east of the park and terminates in the Narrows of the Virgin River about 2 mi north of Temple of Sinawava. More than half of the trek is outside park boundaries. Access the canyon via a dirt road (North Fork Road) approximately 4 mi east of Zion's East Entrance on Route 9. Similar to the Narrows, you walk in the river and along its rocky shoreline through increasingly steep, narrow, and waterlogged terrain. Ropes and rappelling equipment are required, as are permits (which are available at visitor centers or from the National Park Service's Web site). ⊠ *11.5 mi north of Rte. 9 on North Fork Rd., Zion Canyon* ☞Difficult.

The Subway (Left Fork). Start at the Wildcat Canyon Trailhead, near Lava Point, and emerge at the Left Fork trailhead, both along Kolob Terrace Road. The trek requires that you carry at least 60 feet of rope; swim through deep, debris-filled pools; and have extensive route-finding experience. The reward is a subway tunnel-like rock formation that has been carved by the river. Descend from the arid plateau and emerge in a lush riverbed lined with trees and impossibly high cliffs. Other highlights include a 30-foot slab of dinosaur tracks, numerous side canyons, and the volcanic rock fields at Left Fork trailhead. ✉ *Wildcat Canyon Trailhead on Kolob Terrace Rd., 17 mi north of Rte. 9, Kolob Canyons* ⚲ *Difficult.*

West Rim Trail. Hike from Lava Point to the Grotto (about 13½ mi) along the high plateaus west of the Virgin River. Temperatures here may be 10 to 15 degrees cooler than those in Zion Canyon due to the altitude, but your exposure to the sun may be greater, so prepare appropriately. Ten campsites along the way allow you to break up this hike, but permits are required. ✉ *Lava Point Trailhead on Kolob Terrace Rd., 20 mi north of Rte. 9, Kolob Canyons* ⚲ *Difficult.*

Zion Narrows. "From the Top" means shuttling out to Chamberlain Ranch northeast of the park and following the canyon for 16 mi to the temple of Sinawava. It can be done as a day hike, but most hikers stop at one of 12 backcountry campsites in the park. You'll have to rappel down 12-foot waterfalls, wander through miles of river, and explore multiple side canyons. On the plus side, it's all downhill! Ropes and rappelling equipment are required, as are backcountry permits. Several local outfitters offer shuttle service to Chamberlain Ranch; if you're driving yourself, turn left after you cross the Virgin River and drive ¼ mi to Chamberlain Ranch. Drive ½ mi farther and park just before road crosses river. Follow this road for 3 mi on foot and enter river when road ends. ✉ *Approx. 18 mi north of Rte. 9 on park's east side, Zion Valley* ⚲ *Difficult.*

EDUCATIONAL PROGRAMS

CLASSES & SEMINARS

Zion Canyon Field Institute. Throughout the year, Zion Canyon becomes a classroom with seminars on edible plants, geology, photography, adobe-brick making, or any number of other educational programs. The Zion Canyon Field Institute is the educational wing of the Zion Natural History Association and conducts some events in the nature center and throughout the park. ZCFI also conducts workshops at nearby Cedar Breaks National Monument and Pipe Spring National Monument. Classes are limited to small groups;

reserve ahead to assure placement. ☎ *800/635–3959* ⊕*www.zionpark.org* ⊠ *$12–$225.*

ZION NATURAL HISTORY ASSOCIATION. Since 1931, the Zion Natural History Association (ZNHA) has supported education, research, and other programs not only for Zion National Park, but also for Cedar Breaks National Monument and Pipe Spring National Monument. Financial support by ZNHA members combines with the sales from bookstores to provide the parks with approximately $400,000 in aid annually. The educational arm of ZNHA is the Zion Canyon Field Institute (ZCFI), which provides dozens of hands-on seminars each year.

RANGER PROGRAMS

Evening Programs. Held each evening in campground amphitheaters and in Zion Lodge, these entertaining 45-minute ranger-led programs inform you on subjects such as geology and history. You may learn about the bats that swoop through the canyons at night, the surreptitious ways of the mountain lion, or how plants and animals adapt to life in the desert. Programs may include a slide show or audience participation. ☎ *435/772–3256.*

Junior Ranger Program. Kids ages 6 to 12 can have fun learning about plants, animals, geology, and archaeology through this free series of hands-on activities, games, and hikes. They can earn a certificate, pin, and patch by attending one session of the Junior Ranger Program at the Zion Nature Center and one other ranger-led activity in the park. Children 5 or younger can earn a Junior Ranger decal by completing an activity sheet available at the Zion Canyon Visitor Center. Kids can earn a Junior Ranger badge by working through an activity booklet (available at the Zion Canyon and Kolob Canyons visitor centers) during their visit to Zion. Kids need to sign up for Junior Ranger programs at the Zion Nature Center half an hour before they begin. ⊠ *Zion Nature Center, near South Campground entrance, ½ mi north of south entrance, Zion Valley* ☎*435/772–3256*

ZION NATURE CENTER. Rededicated by First Lady Barbara Bush in 2007, the Nature Center serves as the hub of Junior Rangers program. Established in 1974, Zion Junior Rangers program is one of the park service's oldest children's programs. Junior Rangers participate in a bevy of educational activities to learn about the history, geology, and ecology of Zion. Housed in a former cafeteria building designed by legendary architect Gilbert Stanley Underwood, the building is worth a look in its own right.

Morning & Afternoon Hikes. These 1- to 2-mi ranger-led walks can greatly enhance your understanding of the geology, wildlife, and history of Zion National Park. Each park ranger selects a favorite destination, which may change daily. Inquire at the Zion Canyon Visitor Center or check park bulletin boards for locations and times, which vary throughout the year. Wear sturdy footgear and bring a hat, sunglasses, sunscreen, and water.

Shuttle Tours. To learn about the geology, ecology, and history of Zion Canyon, join a park ranger for a two-hour narrated tour by shuttle bus. These free tours depart from the Zion Canyon Visitor Center and travel to Temple of Sinawava. You can make several stops along the way to take photographs and hear park interpretation from the ranger. Tour times are posted at the Zion Canyon Visitor Center, which is also where you can pick up your free but mandatory tour tickets. ⊠ *Zion Canyon Visitor Center, at south entrance, Zion Canyon* ☎*435/772–3256* ☉*May–Sept., daily.*

ARTS & ENTERTAINMENT

As good as their Mexican food is, the **Bit & Spur Restaurant and Saloon** (⊠ *1212 Zion Park Blvd., Springdale* ☎ *435/772–3498*) is also known as the premier place to see live music in southern Utah. Many touring rock, blues, and reggae bands go out of their way to play here.

You can see a quarter-century of work by **Michael Fatali Photography** (⊠ *145 S. Zion Park Blvd., Springdale* ☎ *435/772–2422* ⊕ *www.fatali.com*), a Zion institution, at this gallery. Soaring, scenic, and dramatically lighted, Fatali's landscapes from Zion, Bryce, and surroundings are stunning.

The **O.C. Tanner Amphitheater** (⊠ *Lion Blvd., Springdale* ☎*435/652–7994* ⊕ *www.dixie.edu/tanner*) is set amid huge sandstone boulders at the base of the enormous red cliffs spilling south from Zion National Park. Operated by Dixie State College, live concerts are held most weekends in summer, when everything from local country-music bands to the

Utah Symphony Orchestra take to the stage. Tickets are $10 unless otherwise noted.

The Springdale artist community sees itself an emerging arts community, inspired by the more famous havens of Santa Fe and Sedona. It started here at **Worthington Gallery** (✉ *789 Zion Park Blvd., Springdale* ☎ *800/626–9973*) in 1980 by a single potter in a pioneer-era home near the mouth of Zion Canyon, Worthington Gallery now features more than 20 artists who create in clay, metal, glass, paint, and more. Lyman Whitaker's wind sculptures, Jim Stewart's Orient-meets-southwest ceramics, and Jim Jones's landscapes are particularly noteworthy.

☾ **Zion Canyon Giant Screen Theatre** (✉ *145 Zion Park Blvd., Springdale* ☎ *435/772–2400 or 888/256–3456* ⊕ *www.zioncanyontheatre.com*) has a six-story-high screen that shows the 40-minute film *Zion Canyon–Treasure of the Gods*, an Imax film that takes you on an adventure through Zion and other points in canyon country. Other films, including Hollywood features, are also regularly shown here. Admission is $8, and the theater is open daily from April through October from 11 to 8, with more limited hours from November through March.

SHOPPING

Springdale is the gateway to Zion National Park from the south and offers most services including grocery store, service stations, post office, restaurants, and outfitting companies. There are numerous bookstores, art galleries, cafés, and souvenir shops to while away your time as well. If you're hitting the road or the trail, many restaurants will pack lunches for you on request.

IN THE PARK

At the **Fred Harvey Trading Company Gift Shop** (✉ *Zion Lodge, Zion Canyon Scenic Dr., 3¼ mi north of Canyon Junction, Zion Valley* ☎ *435/772–7700*), in Zion Lodge, discover many local treasures, including Native American jewelry, handmade gifts, books, and other souvenirs.

The **Zion Canyon Visitor Center Bookstore** (✉ *Zion Canyon Visitor Center, at south entrance to park, Zion Valley* ☎ *800/635–3959*) sells books, maps, puzzles, posters, postcards, videos, and even water bottles. It's a comprehensive shop.

IN SPRINGDALE

Canyon Offerings (⊠ *933 Zion Park Blvd., Springdale* ☏ *435/772–3456 or 800/788–2443*) sells some of Zion's snazziest souvenirs. It's packed with gifts for mom, grandma, and the kids, and has one of the best selections of handcrafted jewelry in the region.

Juniper Berry Books (⊠ *868 Zion Park Blvd., Springdale* ☏ *435/772–0990*) offers new and used novels, regional interest, maps, guidebooks, audio books, and more. Special orders are welcome if you're staying in town long enough to receive them.

Manzanita Trading Co. (⊠ *205 Zion Park Blvd., Springdale* ☏ *435/772–0123* ⊕ *manzanitatrading.home.att.net*), adjacent to Café Soleil, showcases pottery and other fine ceramics, jewelry, and artworks created exclusively by Utah artists. So grab a beverage and enjoy the colorful work by local artists. Odds are owner Debra Proball will be on hand to answer any questions you may have.

Sol Foods Market & Deli (⊠ *95 Zion Park Blvd., Springdale* ☏ *435/772–0277* ⊕ *www.solfoods.com*) is Springdale's largest grocery store. It's also adjacent to the Giant Screen Theatre, just outside the park entrance. Pick up food, beverages, and supplies for your excursion, or stay for a quick healthful meal. Because of Springdale's remote location, you should expect prices to be higher than in typical city markets. For more elaborate shopping needs, shop in Hurricane, Cedar City, or St. George.

Sundancer Books (⊠ *975 Zion Park Blvd., Springdale* ☏ *435/772–3400* ⊕ *www.sundancerbooks.blogspot.com*), a 2008 addition to the Springdale shopping (and reading) scene, has big windows that invite you in, not to mention a nice selection of books, local art, and knickknacks to keep you around for a while.

Zion Outdoor Gear & Clothing (⊠ *868 Zion Park Blvd., Springdale* ☏ *435/772–0630*) has the town's best selection of apparel, shoes, and equipment for any outdoor adventure. Leading brands like Outdoor Research, Prana, Camelbak, Black Diamond, and Kavu are featured. Prices are reasonable.

Where to Eat & Stay in Zion

INCLUDING SPRINGDALE, ORDERVILLE & VIRGIN

WORD OF MOUTH

"[In] Zion, [stay at] the Desert Pearl or call the lodge in Zion NP daily for cancellations. Odds are your persistence will be rewarded with a room or cabin. Cancellations are common."

—Peterboy

By Steve
Pastorino
THE GATEWAY TO ZION IS THE TOWN OF SPRINGDALE,
which has more services and amenities—including a broad
spectrum of resorts, boutique inns, and bed-and-breakfasts—than ever. What's more, although it's in middle of
the desert, with midsummer temperatures often in the
100-plus °F range, there's a truly impressive abundance
of fresh fish, flavorful natural ingredients, and vegetarian
options in Springdale's restaurants.

Such growth is a blessing and a curse. On the one hand,
part of Zion's appeal is that it has far more room-and-board
options than Bryce Canyon—hence, the nearly 3 million
annual visitors. On the other hand, the area has lost some of
its charm while seeing an increase in traffic and prices. Still,
as night falls on the Virgin River valley floor, the temperatures drop, the animals emerge, and you realize why this
area has been a sanctuary since pre-Columbian times.

WHERE TO EAT

The Red Rock Grill is the only full-service restaurant
in the only full-service accommodation (Zion Lodge) in
Zion National Park. It offers the warm stone-and-timber
comfort that make the West's best park lodges such important stops.

In Springdale, dawn breaks with the smell of fresh-roasted
coffee and fresh-baked pastries at multiple coffee shops
and restaurants. Café Oscar's (for huevos rancheros) and
the Springdale Fruit Company (for panini) are among the
interesting choices here. To the east, Mt. Carmel Junction
is the first community you reach off the park entrance
road—it's a one stop-sign sort of place without the charm
or choices of Springdale.

Utah doesn't have a signature cuisine, per se; rather, its
restaurants borrow from a number of sources. American
dishes are most common, followed closely by those with
Mexican or Southwestern influences. Because this is a conservative state, don't presume a restaurant serves beer, much
less wine or cocktails, especially in smaller towns. Also,
many places may be closed on Sunday.

Almost every restaurant is family-friendly, and dress is
hiker-casual. Prices are reasonable, though they inch higher
in and near the national park. Be advised that although
Zion is increasingly a four-season community, many busi-

nesses still shutter their doors through the coldest months (January and February).

WHAT IT COSTS AT DINNER				
¢	$	$$	$$$	$$$$
under $8	$8–$12	$13–$20	$21–$30	over $30

Restaurant prices are per person for a main course at dinner and do not include any service charges or taxes.

IN THE PARK

¢ ×**Castle Dome Café & Snack Bar.** *American.* This small fast-food restaurant, right next to the Zion Lodge shuttle stop and adjoining the gift shop, defines convenience. Hikers on the go can grab a banana or a sandwich here; those with a more leisurely approach can while away an hour with ice cream on the sunny patio. ⊠*Zion Canyon Scenic Dr., 3¼ mi north of Canyon Junction* ☎*435/772-7700* ⊕*www.zionlodge.com* ⊟*AE, D, DC, MC, V*

$$ ×**Red Rock Grill at Zion Lodge.** *Southwestern.* Reservations are still required in Zion National Park's only full-service restaurant. But once you're inside this cozy eatery, however, everything is strictly casual. Although the heavy-beam "park-i-tecture" construction is fairly recent (the original building burned to the ground in the 1960s), you step into the past via photos that chronicle the park's 100 years. For dinner, pasta Zion (pasta with sautéed vegetables in white wine reduction), Santa Fe flatiron steak (topped with pico de gallo, onion straws, and blue cheese), and chipotle tilapia reflect the regional influence. A modest wine list includes a dozen varieties by the glass. Lunch options consist of sandwiches, salads, and a "taco bar" that has free-range beef among its selections. You can also get breakfast here. Weather permitting, enjoy your meal on the patio overlooking the lodge's front lawn. ⊠*Zion Canyon Scenic Dr., 3¼ mi north of Canyon Junction* ☎*435/772-7760* ⊕*www.zionlodge.com* ⌂*Reservations essential* ⊟*AE, D, DC, MC, V.*

PICNIC AREAS IN THE PARK
Whether in the cool of Zion Canyon or on a point overlooking the drama of Kolob Canyons, a picnic can be a relaxing break during a busy day of exploring.

☾ ✕**The Grotto.** A shady lunch retreat with lots of amenities—drinking water, fire grates, picnic tables, and restrooms—makes the Grotto ideal for families. A short walk takes you to Zion Lodge, where you can pick up snacks and/or convenience foods at the Castle Dome Café. ⊠*Zion Canyon Scenic Dr., 3½ mi north of Canyon Junction.*

✕**Kolob Canyons Viewpoint.** Nearly 100% of travelers along Interstate 15 from Las Vegas to Salt Lake overlook this short drive a few hundred yards from the highway. The reward is a beautiful view of Kolob's "finger" canyons from about six picnic tables spread out beneath the trees. The parking lot has plenty of space, a pit toilet, and an overlook with a display pointing out canyon features. Restrooms and drinking water are available at the Kolob Canyons Visitor Center. ⊠*Kolob Canyons Rd., 5 mi from Kolob Canyons Visitor Center.*

☾ ✕**Zion Nature Center.** Rededicated by First Lady Laura Bush in 2007, the Zion Nature Center is the seasonal home to Junior Ranger programs, museum exhibits, and a picnic area. Restrooms and drinking water are available in season; otherwise, use the amenities at the South Campground. ⊠*Near entrance to South Campground, ½ mi north of south entrance* ☎*435/772–3256.*

IN SPRINGDALE

$$–$$$ Fodors Choice ✕**Bit & Spur Restaurant and Saloon.** *Mexican.* This restaurant has been a legend in Utah for 20 years. The seasonal menu lists familiar Mexican dishes, but the kitchen also gets creative. Try the chilli-rubbed *bistek asado* (roast beef), the sweet potato and pork tamales, or the chipotle shrimp pasta. The chips, salsa, and margaritas (six varieties by the glass or pitcher) are tempting in their own right. When the weather is nice, you can eat outside and enjoy the lovely grounds and views. ⊠*1212 Zion Park Blvd., Springdale* ☎*435/772–3498* ⊕*www.bitandspur.com* ⊟*AE, D, MC, V* ⊗*No lunch.*

$–$$ ✕**Café Oscar's.** *Southwestern.* The Southwestern menu has dishes made with fresh chicken and beef as well as New Mexico chilies and delicious salsa. And Oscar's serves huevos rancheros all day long, which, in this case, means from 8 AM to "2 hours past sunset." A great vibe, a creative chef, and fresh ingredients make this a local favorite. ⊠*948 Zion Park Blvd., Springdale* ☎*435/772–3232* ⊟*AE, D, MC, V.*

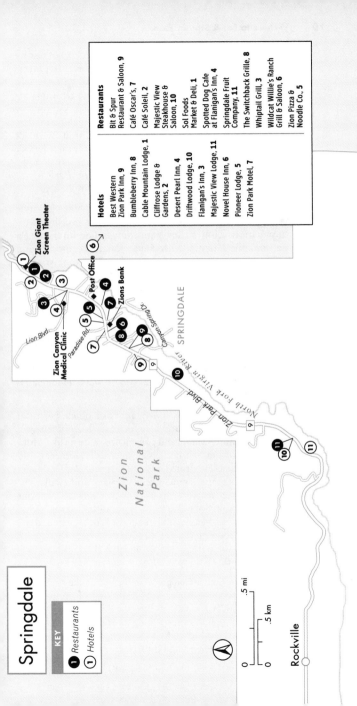

Springdale

KEY
- ① Restaurants
- ① Hotels

Hotels
Best Western
Zion Park Inn, **9**
Bumbleberry Inn, **8**
Cable Mountain Lodge, **1**
Cliffrose Lodge &
Gardens, **2**
Desert Pearl Inn, **4**
Driftwood Lodge, **10**
Flanigan's Inn, **3**
Majestic View Lodge, **11**
Novel House Inn, **6**
Pioneer Lodge, **5**
Zion Park Motel, **7**

Restaurants
Bit & Spur
Restaurant & Saloon, **9**
Café Oscar's, **7**
Café Soleil, **2**
Majestic View
Steakhouse &
Saloon, **10**
Sol Foods
Market & Deli, **1**
Spotted Dog Cafe
at Flanigan's Inn, **4**
Springdale Fruit
Company, **11**
The Switchback Grille, **8**
Whiptail Grill, **3**
Wildcat Willie's Ranch
Grill & Saloon, **6**
Zion Pizza &
Noodle Co., **5**

Zion Giant
Screen Theater

Post Office

Zions Bank

Zion Canyon
Medical Clinic

Lion Blvd.

Paradise Rd.

Zion Canyon Spring Dr.

SPRINGDALE

North Fork Virgin River

Zion Park Blvd.

Zion
National
Park

.5 mi

.5 km

Rockville

$ ✕**Café Soleil.** *Eclectic.* Fresh-brewed specialty coffees by
☾ Desert Sun and gourmet twists on such old breakfast favorites as croissant sandwiches, burritos, and frittatas will
make for a sunny start to your day. It's worth returning for
lunch to try a panini (consider the maple turkey cranberry
with blue cheese), a wrap, a salad, or a 7-inch pizza. The
staff will also package your lunch for the trail. With six
breads and more than a dozen fixings, even the most finicky
sandwich-eaters will find something to their liking. Kids'
portions are available as well. ✉*205 Zion Park Blvd.,
Springdale* ☎*435/772–0505* ═*MC, V* ⊘*No dinner.*

$$$ ✕**Majestic View Steakhouse & Saloon.** *Steak.* This lodge-style
dining room is appropriately named: floor-to-ceiling win-
dows offer Zion Valley panoramas. The interior is a
taxonomist's dream, with giant cougar, elk, moose, and
bear among the animals on display. The sophisticated
menu has such dishes as linguini Portofino (featuring
seafood tossed in a sundried tomato pesto), sautéed scal-
lops and shrimp, and buffalo sirloin steak. Beer from the
on-site Zion Brewery does, indeed, taste like it was hand-
crafted just down the hall; you can try as many as five in
a sampler's flight. A full bar and a list with more than 50
wines from California, Washington, and Italy provide
plenty of other choices. ✉*2400 Zion Park Blvd., Spring-
dale* ☎ *435/772–0665* ⊕*www.majesticviewlodge.com*
═*AE, D, MC, V.*

$ ✕**Sol Foods Market & Deli.** *American.* For a quick, healthful
meal any time of day, stop here for basic groceries as well
as such organic, ethnic, and gourmet food items like Moli-
nari salami from San Francisco, microbrewed beers, and
European cheeses—from gouda to Gorgonzola. Daily spe-
cials include spanakopita, quiche, lasagna, and salads. The
staff can prepare picnic baskets or box lunches for your
day in the park. Sol's also features hand-dipped ice cream,
delicious coffee, video rentals, and free Wi-Fi. On nice days,
enjoy your food on the patio above the Virgin River, with
views into the park. ✉*95 Zion Park Blvd., Springdale*
☎*435/772–0277* ⊕*www.solfoods.com* ═*AE, D, MC, V.*

$$–$$$ ✕**Spotted Dog Cafe at Flanigan's Inn.** *Eclectic.* The restaurant
that's named in honor of the family dog of Springdale's
original settlers counts local trout and pork loin with a
chipotle chili–plum sauce among its entrées. Spotted Dog
also makes the effort to fly in salmon, halibut, tuna, and
other seafood depending on the season. Breakfast is also

served. A sidewalk patio fills quickly. ✉*428 Zion Park Blvd., Springdale* ☎*435/772–3244* ⊕*www.flanigans.com* ▭*AE, DC, MC, V* ✆*No lunch.*

$ ✕**Springdale Fruit Company.** *Contemporary.* Surrounded by apple orchards, this store makes an interesting and healthful stop. The "green" building was inspired by an 1865 Mormon settler's home. Its wood interior is refreshingly old-fashioned, and there's a picnic area in the back. Look for produce, organic products, and fresh-squeezed juices. Sandwiches, trail mixes, and baked goods make heartier snacks. ✉*2491 Zion Park Blvd., Springdale* ☎*435/772–3222* ⊕*www.spring dalefruit.com* ▭*AE, D, MC, V* ✆*No dinner.*

$$$ ✕**The Switchback Grille.** *Contemporary.* Since 1996, the operators of Switchback Grille have worked hard to differentiate their establishment from other Springdale restaurants. They've succeeded thanks to a comfortable dining room with vaulted ceilings; a cigar list; and lunch and dinner menus that include wild game, free-range beef, and wood-fired pizzas. Pasta dishes and pizzas are fairly priced, but steak dishes are among the town's most expensive. Start with artichoke heart and spinach fondue. If you're feeling adventurous, follow it up with the seared ostrich loin; otherwise, consider the Portobello sandwich. Although the Grille is at the Best Western Zion Park Inn, locals often crowd in alongside visitors. ✉*1149 S. Zion Park Blvd., Springdale* ☎*435/772–3700* ⊕*www.switchbackgrille.com* ▭*AE, D, MC, V.*

$$ ✕**Whiptail Grill.** *Southwestern.* Named for a variety of lizard that wanders the nearby canyons, this restaurant in a one-time service station doesn't look like much, but it serves up fantastic Southwestern lunches and dinners. Yellowfin tuna tacos are a specialty; carne asada, burritos, and other spicy dishes round out your choices. ✉*445 Zion Park Blvd., Springdale* ☎*435/772–0283* ▭*D, MC, V* ✆*Closed Dec. and Jan.*

$$ ✕**Wildcat Willie's Ranch Grill & Saloon.** *Southwestern.* This homespun restaurant emulates life on the ranch but is right on Springdale's main drag. You pass through wrought-iron gates before sitting down to enjoy hearty fare. There are paper towels on the tables, drinks in mason jars, a selection of beers (including those from Zion Brewery), and an assortment of homemade pies. Garlic-rosemary chicken breasts, desert crab cakes (salmon with avocado salsa), and blackberry bone-in pork chops are all good entrées. Don't

pass on great sides like grilled sweet corn and garlic mashed potatoes. For a taste of everything, try Sunday brunch. ✉ *897 Zion Park Blvd., Springdale* ☎*435/772–0115* ▭*AE, D, MC, V.*

$ ✕**Zion Pizza & Noodle Co.** *Pizza.* Hearty pizza is a favorite post-hike meal. But if that pizza is good enough, and served up in a converted church, can it become a religious experience? With a dozen signature pies (one for each apostle?), plus calzones, stromboli, and pasta dishes, you'll be hard-pressed not to have a dining revelation here. The Virgin pie features veggies, garlic, and five cheeses; the Tree Hugger has sesame seeds and carrots; and the Cholesterol Hiker makes up for the lack of meat on the first two with pepperoni, Canadian bacon, and Italian sausage. Linguine with peanuts and grilled chicken and spaghetti with homemade marinara sauce are also tempting. The beer garden is open year-round. ✉ *868 Zion Park Blvd., Springdale* ☎*435/ 772–3815* ⊕*www.zionpizzanoodle.com* ▭*No credit cards* ⊙*Closed Dec.–Feb.*

WHERE TO STAY

Since Zion Lodge (the only in-park lodging option) has fewer than 80 rooms, getting a reservation inside the park can be harder than finding a beer at noon on a Sunday in southern Utah. Plan well ahead—by as much as six to nine months, in fact—to ensure a stay in this landmark property near the Virgin River. Designed by Gilbert Stanley Underwood, the original main building was built in 1924–25 and burned down in 1966, but it was rebuilt within 100 days. The rebuilt version, however, was not consistent with the original's look, so the lodge was restored in 1990 to the original style. Some of the adjacent cabins, however, are originals from the late 1920s.

If you can't get a room in the park, try the gateway community of Springdale, which has everything from small motels to quaint bed-and-breakfasts to upscale hotels with modern amenities and riverside rooms. To save the most, consider staying in Hurricane, about 20 mi west of the park. Another 20 mi beyond Hurricane is St. George, a booming community with scores of options for every budget.

WHAT IT COSTS				
¢	$	$$	$$$	$$$$
under $70	$70–$120	$121–$175	$176–$250	over $250

Hotel prices are for a double room in high season and do not include taxes, service charges, or resort fees.

IN THE PARK

$$–$$$ ⊡**Zion Lodge.** Although the original lodge built in 1924–25 burned down in 1966, the rebuilt structure convincingly re-creates the classic look of the old inn. Knotty pine woodwork and log and wicker furnishings accent the lobby. Guest rooms are modern but not fancy. Historic Western-style cabins have gas-log fireplaces. This is a quiet retreat, so there are no TVs; kids can amuse themselves outdoors on the grassy lawns. The lodge is an easy, less than ½-mi walk to trailheads, horseback riding, and, of course, the shuttle stop. Make reservations at least six months in advance (nine months is better). **Pros:** inside the park, on land where Native Americans have dwelled for centuries, inspirational nighttime tranquillity. **Cons:** basic accommodations, lacks amenities, very hard to get a room. ⊠*Zion Canyon Scenic Dr., 3¼ mi north of Canyon Junction, Zion National Park* ☎*435/772–7700* ⊕*www.zionlodge.com* ⤶*75 rooms, 6 suites, 40 cabins* ⎙*In-room: no TV. In-hotel: restaurant* ⊟*AE, D, DC, MC, V.*

IN SPRINGDALE

★ Fodor'sChoice ⊡**Best Western Zion Park Inn.** The spring that led
$ to the naming of Springdale gurgles on the grounds of the
☾ town's largest hotel. Rooms have above-average furnishings and amenities that reflect the standards of the Best Western chain. Cozy sofas, a fireplace, and floor-to-ceiling windows in the lobby open onto a patio perched above a carefully maintained lawn, pool, flower boxes, and the Virgin River. This is an impeccable spot to watch the sun's last rays on the stream below and Watchman cliffs above. The property has nice grounds, two restaurants, a gift shop, a liquor store, and the only elevator in town. **Pros:** good value for the money, plenty of activities, including volleyball, horseshoes, basketball, and a wading pool, allows pets. **Cons:** lacks the charm of a locally owned business, a

little farther from the park entrance than other places. ⊠*1215 Zion Park Blvd., Springdale* ☎*888/772–3200* ⊕*www.zionparkinn.com* ⇆*120 rooms* ⚬*In-room: refrigerator, Wi-Fi. In-hotel: 2 restaurants, 2 pools, laundry facilities, Internet terminal, Wi-Fi, some pets allowed, no-smoking rooms* ⊟*AE, D, MC, V.*

$ ▣**Bumbleberry Inn.** A complete renovation in late 2008 updated this community institution in the center of Springdale and restored its reputation as one of the best values in town. The spacious front lawn is perfect for active children, and the attractive wood-framed lobby with oversize windows is welcoming to road- or trail-weary travelers. Rooms, however, have the basics—nothing extraordinary. Savor the taste (and learn the legend) of bumbleberries in the on-site restaurant, where a panoply of fresh pies awaits. **Pros:** well-maintained, great value, on-site racquetball court. **Cons:** back of the hotel overlooks a cluttered residential area. ⊠*97 Bumbleberry La., Springdale* ☎*435/772–3224* ⊕*www.bumbleberry.com* ⇆*48 rooms* ⚬*In-room: refrigerator, DVD (some), Wi-Fi. In-hotel: restaurant, pool, laundry facilities, Internet terminal, Wi-Fi, no elevator, no-smoking rooms* ⊟*D, MC, V.*

★ **Fodor'sChoice** ▣**Cable Mountain Lodge.** This classy addition to
$$ Springdale's hotels opened in summer 2008. It's on the park boundary and has ample access to the Virgin River with the park's Watchman Campground on the opposite bank. Granite counters, oversize headboards, faux-wood-grain floors, and wood-framed doors give rooms an upscale Western feel. Four Judy Suites (named for the owner's wife) have double-sided fireplaces, with a jetted tub on one side and a king-size bed on the other. **Pros:** so close to the park you can smell campfires, contemporary rooms, riverfront amenities like water tubing. **Cons:** you can't avoid a maze of asphalt (passing a cinema, market, restaurants, and shops) to get here. ⊠*147 Zion Park Blvd., Springdale* ☎*435/772–3366* ⊕*www.cablemountainlodge.com* ⇆*11 rooms, 39 suites* ⚬*In-room: kitchen (some), refrigerator, Wi-Fi. In-hotel: pool, laundry facilities, Wi-Fi, no elevator, no-smoking rooms* ⊟*AE, D, MC, V.*

$$ ▣**Cliffrose Lodge & Gardens.** Flowers adorn 5 acres of attractive, terraced grounds adjacent to the Virgin River and just a short walk from the park entrance as well as a theater, market, restaurants, and other amenities. Rooms are in a half-dozen lodges surrounding a pool, a playground, a

picnic area, fire pits, and paths. The river's gurgling makes for mellow ambient noise. The grounds beckon you outside, while flat-screen high-definition TVs and updated furnishings tempt you to stay in. This place has been family-owned for more than 20 years. **Pros:** great family destination, walking distance to park and more. **Cons:** rooms aren't the cheapest in the area. ⊠ *281 Zion Park Blvd., Springdale* ☎ *435/772–3234* ⊕ *www.cliffroselodge.com* ⇨ *39 rooms* ⌂ *In-room: refrigerator, Wi-Fi. In-hotel: pool, laundry facilities, Wi-Fi, no elevator, no-smoking rooms* ⊟ *AE, D, MC, V.*

★ Fodor'sChoice ⊺**Desert Pearl Inn.** Since 1998, the Palmers have
$$ consistently provided one of Springdale's most memorable lodging experiences just steps from the Virgin River. The six yellow stucco buildings are framed by 19th-century railroad trestle timbers. Inside spacious rooms, oversize windows give ample light to muted desert pastel tones, granite countertops, cathedral ceilings (some units), modern furnishings, and hardwood floors. Riverside and poolside rooms open to patios that are perfect for post-hike lounging, while second-floor units have balconies to enjoy morning coffee or afternoon sunsets. The pool area is exceptionally well landscaped and fully equipped, with a double-size hot tub and a shower-and-restroom block. In-room massage is available for sore hikers. Elements offers pastries, light lunches, convenience items, and art and jewelry from local artisans. **Pros:** attention to detail in well-appointed rooms, consistently good service from experienced staff, no better place to enjoy the river than from the Inn's newest rooms in the "600" building. **Cons:** condolike suites are some of Springdale's most expensive rooms, you may not want to leave. ⊠ *707 Zion Park Blvd., Springdale* ☎ *435/772–8888* ⊕ *www.desertpearl.com* ⇨ *73 rooms* ⌂ *In-room: safe, refrigerator, DVD, Wi-Fi. In-hotel: pool, laundry facilities, Wi-Fi, no-smoking rooms* ⊟ *AE, D, MC, V.*

$$ ⊺**Driftwood Lodge.** Nine acres of grounds adjacent to the Virgin River have made Driftwood Lodge a nice place to wash up on shore for more than 50 years. Since 2006, new ownership has modernized the complex of buildings with more contemporary furnishings including flat-panel high-definition televisions. First-floor rooms have patios and Adirondack chairs—perfect for ending the day below the famous West Temple peak. **Pros:** historic property that has been thoroughly modernized and now features some of the

4

sharpest, cleanest rooms in town, beautiful grounds, one of the few hotels in town that allows pets. **Cons:** on-site restaurant closed in 2008, no river access. ✉*1515 Zion Park Blvd., Springdale* ☎*435/772–3262* ⊕*www.drift woodlodge.net* ➲*42 rooms* ⚬*In-room: refrigerator. In-hotel: pool, Wi-Fi, some pets, no-smoking rooms* ▭*AE, D, MC, V.*

$–$$ 🖫**Flanigan's Inn.** Springdale's only in-hotel spa and salon add a Zen-like tranquillity to this cluster of comfortable cottages. Seemingly carved out of the region's signature red rocks, Flanigan's is a few blocks downhill from the Zion Visitor Center. Rooms are clean, comfortable, and furnished with simple modern pieces. The pool area is small but scenic. The on-property restaurant, the Spotted Dog Cafe, is equally revered for its consistent quality dating back to the 1980s. **Pros:** good location, a refuge where modesty is a positive attribute, on-site massage, yoga, and salon. **Cons:** minimalism is refreshing but also leaves rooms somewhat dark and spartan, some rooms are uncomfortably close to Zion Park Boulevard, families will find more "kid-friendliness" at other properties in town. ✉*428 Zion Park Blvd., Springdale* ☎*435/772–3244* ⊕*www.flanigans. com* ➲*34 rooms* ⚬*In-room: refrigerator (some), DVD, Wi-Fi. In-hotel: restaurant, pool, spa, laundry facilities, Wi-Fi, no-smoking rooms* ▭*AE, D, MC, V.*

$$ 🖫**Majestic View Lodge.** With its heavy-beamed construction, babbling brook in front, and a bevy of animals (both stuffed and in artwork, furnishing, and accents), Majestic View lives up to the "lodge" in its name as well as any property in town. Rooms are spacious, modern, and clean. The first property you'll encounter as you approach Zion National Park from the west, it's easy to bypass the rooms, steak house, taxidermy museum, and gift shop, but you may come back as Majestic View exceeds many of it competitors on all counts. **Pros:** good rooms, better steak house, and best beer in town (Zion Brewing Co. is here). **Cons:** pricey by Springdale standards, the journey through town will cost you time on your way in and out of the park, is it possible to have too many bears in decor? ✉*2400 Zion Park Blvd., Springdale* ☎*435/772–0665* ⊕*www.majestic viewlodge.com* ➲*69 rooms* ⚬*In-room: refrigerator. In-hotel: pool, Wi-Fi, laundry facilities, no-smoking rooms* ▭*AE, D, MC, V.*

$$ Fodor'sChoice ⚏**Novel House Inn.** Fans of literature ranging from C.S. Lewis to Jane Austen, Rudyard Kipling to Louis L'Amour will savor this bed-and-breakfast where each unique room is as compelling as your favorite page-turner. Since 1995 the Clay family has welcomed readers, romance-seekers, and hikers from across the globe. The Kipling room evokes a Raj's quarters. The Walt Whitman room has autumn tones and reflects serenity. The living room is lined with books and parlor games, and the adjacent La Dolce Vita Gallery will sell or maybe even trade you a classic to complete your set. **Pros:** novelty and comfort without kitsch, no two rooms are the same, and the armoires alone are worth asking for a tour of all rooms, one block removed from Zion Park Boulevard, so the nicely maintained grounds are especially peaceful. **Cons:** no kids under 12, so families can't share this place with their aspiring young readers, no refrigerator in your room, although guests are invited to use one off the kitchen. ⊠*73 Paradise Rd., Springdale* ☎*800/711–8400* ⊕*www.novelhouse.com* ⇴*10 rooms* ⌂*In-room: DVD, Wi-Fi. In-hotel: no kids under 12, no-smoking rooms* ⊟*D, MC, V* ⊙*Closed Dec. and Jan.* ⏪*BP.*

$$ ⚏**Pioneer Lodge.** This motel claims to be the oldest building in Springdale, but constant renovations have kept the property up-to-date. Knotty pine beds and faux wood paneling give rooms the pioneer feel, as do the pine railings along exposed walkways. This is the heart of Springdale in many ways, with hikers and backpackers crowding the lobby/bakery/Internet café. The car and foot traffic alongside the sidewalks here feel more like a resort town than the sleepy community of 300-plus people that it is. **Pros:** new air-conditioners, cozy rooms with personal touches. **Cons:** this block of town is as busy as Springdale gets, service can be erratic, this kind of money can deliver better amenities at other hotels in town. ⊠*838 Zion Park Blvd., Springdale* ☎*888/772–3233* ⊕*www.pioneerlodge.com* ⇴*42 rooms* ⌂*In-room: refrigerator, Wi-Fi. In-hotel: restaurant, pool, laundry facilities, Internet terminal, Wi-Fi, no-smoking rooms* ⊟*AE, D, MC, V.*

$ ⚏**Zion Park Motel.** Step into a bygone era in this classic motel where Dodge Darts would look just as at home in the parking lot as today's SUVs. The Young family has operated this clean, simple, 21-room, drive-in motel since 1972, and they take pride in family management and personal touches. All rooms reflect varying degrees of updates, but all are clean and provide basic comfortable sleeping arrangements. The family suite has a full kitchen. A small convenience store adjacent to the lobby helps if you forget something. **Pros:** you can't beat the price in Springdale, catch the shuttle into the park from the motel's parking lot, walk to restaurants and shops. **Cons:** no frills or unique amenities, rooms are small. ⊠ *865 Zion Park Blvd., Springdale* ☎*435/ 772–3251* ⊕*www.zionparkmotel.com* ↵*21 rooms* ♿*Inroom: refrigerator, kitchen (some), Wi-Fi. In-hotel: restaurant, pool, laundry facilities, Internet terminal, Wi-Fi, no-smoking rooms* ⊟*AE, D, MC, V.*

IN ROCKVILLE

$ **Fodor's**Choice 🔲 **Rockville Rose Inn.** For a more affordable change of pace, revel in B&B hospitality at this inn about 4 mi from the south entrance of Zion. A lush green lawn, fruit and nut trees, and four comfortable rooms await you. Onsite owners take pride in attending to all guest needs, including providing a full-cooked breakfast daily. **Pros:** nice property, wonderful hosts in a sleepy village. **Cons:** there are many options closer to the park, Rockville offers almost no other services. ⊠ *125 E. Main St., Rockville* ☎*435/ 772–0800* ⊕*www.rockvilleroseinn.com* ↵*4 rooms* ♿*Inroom: refrigerator, Wi-Fi. In-hotel: no-smoking rooms* ⊟*AE, D, MC, V* ◉|*BP.*

WHERE TO CAMP

Two primary campgrounds within Zion National Park are family-friendly, convenient, and generally pleasant, but in the high season they do fill up fast. Don't expect solitude as both South Campground and Watchman Campground host hundreds of campers every night in high season. In midsummer, Zion's searing heat can leave the campgrounds fairly deserted in midday. Flock to the river, nearby canyons, and/or higher altitude to find some relief.

Backcountry camping in the park is an option for overnight backpackers, but make sure to get a permit at the Zion Canyon or Kolob Canyon Visitor Center. The primitive Lava Point Campground has no water and is closed in winter and spring but is a rarity as a free place to stay inside the National Park. Its six sites are first-come, first-served.

Outside of the park, there are options to the north, east, and west of the park. Regardless, your best bet is to reserve ahead of time whenever possible. Private campgrounds cater to families, often featuring amenities such as playground, showers, picnic areas and, in some cases, swimming pools.

WHAT IT COSTS				
¢	$	$$	$$$	$$$$
under $8	$8–$14	$15–$20	$21–$25	over $25

Camping prices are for campsites that include a tent area, fire pit, bear-proof food-storage box, picnic table; potable water and pit toilets or restrooms will be nearby.

4

IN THE PARK

$$ ⛺ **South Campground.** All the sites here are under big cottonwood trees, granting campers some relief from the summer sun. The campground operates on a first-come, first-served basis, and sites are usually filled before noon each day during high season. Many of the sites are suitable for either tents or RVs, although there are no hookups. Reservations not accepted. ⊠ *Rte. 9, ½ mi north of south entrance* 🕾 *435/772–3256* 🛏 *127 sites* ⚘ *Flush toilets, dump station, drinking water, fire grates, picnic tables, no showers* ⊟ *No credit cards* ⊘ *Mid-Mar.–Nov.*

¢ ⛺ **Lava Point Campground.** This little-known gem of a campground is within park limits but accessible by car only by driving the length of Kolob Terrace Road, which intersects Route 9 in the town of Virgin, 13.6 mi east of the park entrance. Follow Kolob Terrace Road 20 mi north, then turn right at the campground sign. The sparsely maintained road may be impassable after heavy rains. Your journey is rewarded with six peaceful, tree-shaded campsites at 7,800 feet above sea level (and thus about 10°F cooler on average than the Zion Park Visitor Center). These primitive campsites have fire pits and picnic tables but no potable water. There is *no* charge to camp here. The adjacent trailheads offer access to the West Rim Trail and Wildcat Canyon. ⊠ *Access road off Kolob Terrace Rd.* 🕾 *435/772–3256* 🛏 *6 sites, no hookups* ⚘ *Pit toilets, fire grates, picnic tables* ⊘ *June–Oct., weather permitting.*

$$ ⛺ **Watchman Campground.** This sprawling campground on the Virgin River operates on a reservation system between April and October, and it fills up quickly, so plan ahead.

CAMPING IN ZION AND SPRINGDALE

Campground Name	Total # of Sites	# of RV sites	# of hook-ups	Drive-to sites	Hike-to sites	Flush toilets	Pit toilets	Drinking water	Showers	Fire grates/pits	Swimming	Boat access	Playground	Dump station	Ranger station	Public telephone	Reservations Possible	Daily fee per site	Dates open
Lava Point South Campground	6	0		Y			Y			Y								Free	Jun-Oct
Watchman Campground	127	127		Y		Y		Y		Y				Y				$16	Mar-Nov
Watchman Campground	164	95	95	Y		Y		Y	Y	Y				Y	Y	Y	Y	$16-$20	Y/R
Zion Canyon Campground & RV Park	220	110	110	Y		Y		Y	Y	Y			Y	Y		Y	Y	$25-$30	Y/R
Zion River Resort RV Park & Campground	126	114	11	Y		Y		Y	Y	Y	Y		Y	Y			Y	$36-$45	Y/R

Y/R = year-round   ** = Summer Only

With five loops of campsites, the campground allows everyone from tent-toting hikers to RVers to rub shoulders. Loops C and D are tent-only and quieter than the RV area. Several group sites can accommodate as many as 50 people each, turning this campground into one of the rowdier places to stay. An amphitheater hosts nightly ranger talks on topics from the park's flora and fauna to tall tales and legends. Walk to the Zion Canyon Visitor Center and to the Pa'rus trail. Sometimes you can get same-day reservations, but don't count on it. ⊠*Access road off Zion Canyon Visitor Center parking lot* ☏*435/772–3256, 877/444–6777 reservations* ⊕*www.recreation.gov* ⇌*164 sites, 95 with hookups* ⚴*Group sites, flush toilets, partial hookups (electric), dump station, drinking water, fire grates, picnic tables, no showers* ▭*D, MC, V* ☉*Apr.–Oct., weather permitting.*

IN SPRINGDALE & VIRGIN

$$$–
$$$$ ⚴ **Zion Canyon Campground & RV Park.** In Springdale about a half-mile from the south entrance to the park, this campground is surrounded on three sides by the canyon's rock formations. Many of the sites are on the river. ⊠*479 Zion Park Blvd., Springdale* ☏*435/772–3237* ⊕*www.zioncamp. com/rv_park.html* ⇌*110 RV sites, 110 tent sites* ⚴*Flush toilets, full hookups, dump station, drinking water, guest laundry, showers, fire grates, picnic tables, food service, electricity, public telephone, general store, play area, swimming (river)* ▭*D, MC, V.*

$$$$ ⚴ **Zion River Resort RV Park & Campground.** Approximately 12 mi from the South Entrance to the park, this "RV resort" is clean, modern, and spacious. It offers something for everyone, from cabins to tent sites to 70-foot pull-through sites. Many of these are on the river. There are also cabins, which range from $87 to $99 per night (you supply bedding). ⊠ *551 E. Hwy. 9, Virgin* ☏*800/838–8594* ⊕*www. zionriverresort.com* ⇌*114 RV sites, 11 tent sites, 3 cabins* ⚴*Swimming pool, spa, flush toilets, full hookups, dump station, drinking water, guest laundry, showers, fire grates, picnic tables, convenience store, electricity, public telephone, general store, play area, free Wi-Fi* ▭*D, MC, V.*

Exploring
Bryce Canyon

WORD OF MOUTH

"In my opinion—and others may disagree—Bryce was so unusual, so unlike other places I've been to! And I was there after Zion. I would not miss the delicate beauty of Bryce."

—FainaAgain

By Steve
Pastorino

THE SMALLER AND YOUNGER SIBLING TO ZION NATIONAL PARK, Bryce nonetheless is a favorite among Utah's five national parks. Within approximately 56 square mi (one fourth the size of Zion and one-tenth the size of Canyonlands) lie three distinct temperate zones, tens of millions of years of geological history, a scenic drive, more than a dozen trails, and countless species of birds, animals, and flora.

The park is named for hard-luck pioneer rancher Ebenezer Bryce, who famously remarked that Bryce is "a hell of a place to lose a cow." He departed the valley below the canyon five years after arriving (for Arizona), but not before laying the groundwork for a flourishing agricultural community.

The land he left behind captures the imagination and the heart with its fanciful "hoodoos," best viewed at sunrise or sunset, when the light plays off the red rock. In geological terms, Bryce is actually an amphitheater, not a canyon. The hoodoos in the amphitheater took on their unusual shapes because the top layer of rock—"cap rock"—is harder than the layers below it. If erosion undercuts the soft rock beneath the cap too much, the hoodoo will tumble.

The high plateau, with the visitor center, scenic drive, and Ruby's Inn is named Paunsaugunt, the Paiute Indian word for "home of the beaver." With much of the plateau at an elevation of more than 8,000 feet, it's covered by hardy pines, inhabited by deer and small mammals, and surrounded by clean air. Its rim gives way to an otherworldly landscape that attracts more than a million visitors per year.

A perfect day in Bryce consists of a leisurely exploration of its scenic drive, a brisk hike into the amphitheater, and an educational experience with a ranger or at the visitor center. Given additional time, further explorations by foot, bicycle, skis, or snowshoes will only enhance your memories.

SO WHAT'S A HOODOO? [*hoo'doo*] **1.** *n.* **A pinnacle or odd-shape rock left standing by the forces of erosion. 2.** *v.* **To cast a spell or cause bad luck. 3. Voodoo. Ask park rangers and you will get different answers. Sometimes we think they like to tease visitors with playful stories, but fact is, the name is attributed to various times and sources. Certainly it rolls off the tongue, and is more fun for kids to say than, "Hey Mom—check out that eroded rock formation!"**

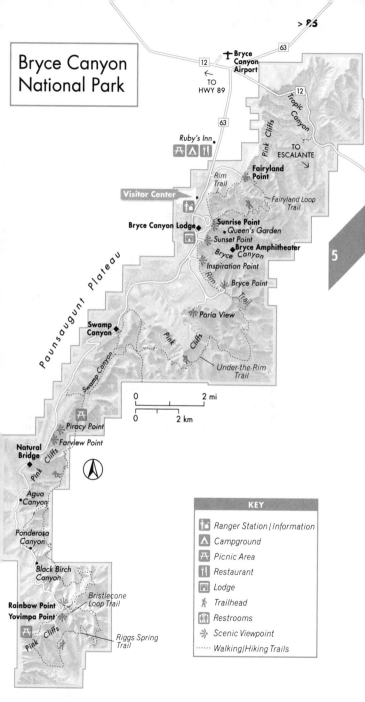

Bryce Canyon National Park

> 9.5

Bryce Canyon Airport

TO HWY 89

TO ESCALANTE

Ruby's Inn

Fairyland Point

Rim Trail

Visitor Center

Fairyland Loop Trail

Pink Cliffs

Tropic Canyon

Bryce Canyon Lodge

Sunrise Point
Queen's Garden
Sunset Point
Bryce Amphitheater
Bryce Canyon

Inspiration Point

Bryce Point

Rim Trail

Paria View

Paunsaugunt Plateau

Swamp Canyon

Pink Cliffs

Under-the-Rim Trail

Swamp Canyon

0   2 mi

0   2 km

Piracy Point

Farview Point

Natural Bridge

Pink Cliffs

Agua Canyon

Ponderosa Canyon

Black Birch Canyon

Bristlecone Loop Trail

Rainbow Point
Yovimpa Point

Pink Cliffs

Riggs Spring Trail

5

KEY

- 🛈 Ranger Station/Information
- 🛆 Campground
- 🪧 Picnic Area
- 🍴 Restaurant
- 🛏 Lodge
- 🚶 Trailhead
- 🚻 Restrooms
- ✳ Scenic Viewpoint
- ----- Walking/Hiking Trails

BRYCE CANYON BEST BETS

■ **Get into the zone(s):**
Bryce Canyon's elevation
range—2,000 feet—is such
that it spans three climatic
zones: spruce/fir forest,
ponderosa pine forest, and
pinyon pine/juniper forest.
The result is a park rich
in biodiversity.

■ **Bryce Amphitheater:**
This one-of-a-kind geological
wonder is the heart of the
park. Choose a variety of
viewpoints, at different times
of the day, and take a least
one short hike below the rim
to fully appreciate its breath-
taking beauty.

■ **Scenic drive:** Don't rush
through this 18-mi drive.
Every viewpoint offers a stunning view with a unique perspective on millions of years
of geological evolution.

■ **Mossy Cave:** This less-
visited nook of the park
(accessed by State Highway
12) offers a close-up perspective on hoodoos from
the bottom-up—without any
difficult hiking.

■ **Winter fun:** Imagine a
crisp layer of snowy icing on
Bryce's memorable horizon.
Then, step into cross-country
skis or snowshoes for a brisk
winter workout.

PLANNING YOUR TIME

BRYCE CANYON IN ONE DAY

Begin your day at the **visitor center** just past the park
entrance. Read through *The Hoodoo* newspaper, watch
the movie about the park, and speak with a ranger to get
an overview of the park. Choose a ranger-led hike or talk
(for adults and/or kids); it will be the most interesting and
informative 60 minutes you spend in the park.

Presuming you have the better part of a day, beat the
crowds by driving all the way to the south end of the park
and get your first look at the canyon at **Rainbow Point**. A
short, rolling hike along the **Bristlecone Loop Trail** at Rainbow Point rewards you with spectacular views and a cool
walk through a forest of bristlecone pines. On a clear day,
you'll be able to see south to the Grand Canyon, east to
Grand Staircase National Monument and west across the
Paunsaugunt plateau.

Start working your way back to the Bryce Point. Don't feel
like you have to hit every viewpoint, but recommended
stops should include **Agua Canyon, Natural Bridge,** and **Farview
Point**. Allow two to three hours for the drive, and save a half-

day for the Bryce Amphitheater. Begin your explorations
of the heart of the park at **Bryce Canyon Lodge** or **General
Store** if you need to eat or replenish snacks. Enjoy a stroll
along the relaxing **Rim Trail**, or drop down into the canyon
on one of the park's signature short hikes.

The easiest route into the amphitheater is the **Queen's Garden Trail** at Sunrise Point. If you're a little more ambitious,
take the steep switchbacks of the **Navajo Loop** to **Wall Street**.
Remember that almost all Bryce hikes feature a sharp descent
into the canyon at the outset, which unfortunately means a
rigorous climb to exit. Most of the plateau is at or above
8,000 feet, so be aware of the thin air and risk of sunburn.

End your day with dinner at **Bryce Canyon Lodge** (you'll want
to have made your reservations that morning). Try to time
sunset to be at an overlook; **Inspiration Point, Sunset Point,**
and **Bryce Point** each offer memorable vistas.

As you leave the park, stop at **Ruby's Inn** for Native American jewelry, souvenirs, hand-dipped ice-cream cones, or
any other supplies for the road.

BRYCE CANYON IN THREE DAYS

Your choice of lodging will help you define three unforgettable days in Bryce. For the consummate historical experience, reserve (well in advance!) a cabin at **Bryce Canyon Lodge**.
For starry-sky nights and a likely visit from mule deer, choose
either campground in the park. For a few more amenities, pick
an RV site, tepee, tent, or standard room at **Ruby's Inn.**

As dawn breaks on your first day, consult with rangers at
the **visitor center** and choose a Geology Talk, Ranger Hike,
or Astronomy program that suits your schedule. Then head
into the canyon at **Sunrise Point,** combining the **Queen's
Garden** and **Navajo** trails. You can see Queen Victoria,
Thor's Hammer, and Wall Street: three of the park's most
famous icons. Relax and recover from this moderate hike
with the 18-mi scenic drive, stopping to see **Agua Canyon,
Natural Bridge,** and **Bryce Point.** Wherever you are on the
plateau, keep your eyes open for deer, prairie dogs, and
dozens of bird species.

On Day 2, skip the crowds by descending into the canyon
for a half-day hike. **Peekaboo Loop** (three to four hours)
takes you to see the Wall of Windows; **Fairyland Loop** (four
to five hours) takes you to Tower Bridge and China Wall;
Agua Canyon (four to five hours) gives you a taste of the
famed Under the Rim Trail and a view of Natural Bridge

The Drive

As nearly every lookout along the Bryce Canyon Scenic Drive is on the East side of the Main Road, rangers recommend driving the length of the park north-to-south without stopping; if you do that, it will be easier to pull off at the lookouts as you drive north again. There are several dozen places to stop, each offering a different perspective, geologic feature, trailhead, or mere resting point. Trying to identify the "best" places to stop is a matter of opinion, but here are three we think you shouldn't miss:

■ Rainbow/Yovimpa Point, the southernmost—and highest—point in the park. Gaze to the west and see the Dixie National Forest. To the south, see the Grand Canyon on a clear day. To the east, see Horse Mountain and Grand Staircase–Escalante National Monument.

■ Natural Bridge. Utahans take their arches seriously (ask one how many they've seen in person). You can start your own personal count with this quick, easy, and breathtaking stop.

■ Bryce Point. Follow the short trail to the overlook and drink in a near-360-degree panorama of majestic cliffs and hoodoos. Nowhere else in the park has such a broad spectrum.

Be careful pulling into and out of lookouts. Whether they are large, striped parking lots or roadside shoulders, be alert for moving cars, crossing pedestrians, and the occasional animal as well.

from below. End your day with dinner at **Bryce Canyon Lodge** (you'll want to have made your reservations that morning). Try to time sunset to be at an overlook, **Inspiration Point, Sunset Point,** or **Bryce Point,** each of which offers memorable vistas.

On your final day, savor the perspectives from **Fairyland Point** or Bryce Point, then return to **Highway 12** (a national scenic byway). If you're headed west, spend an hour exploring **Red Canyon** (10 mi from the turnoff for Bryce) in the Dixie National Forest; the 0.8-mi **Birds Eye Trail** is a kid-friendly hike from the informative visitor center. Save room for a slice of homemade pie at Bryce Canyon Pines restaurant and motel. If you're headed east, hike to **Mossy Cave** (within Bryce Canyon National Park but accessible only from Highway 12), a short 1-mi round-trip that showcases Bryce's floral diversity and a small waterfall. Grab dinner or hand-dipped ice cream at the ice-cream shop adjacent to Clarke's restaurant in Tropic.

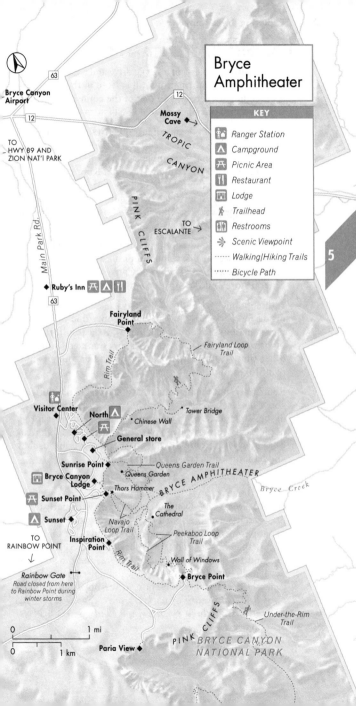

Bryce Amphitheater

KEY

🏚	Ranger Station
⛺	Campground
🪧	Picnic Area
🍴	Restaurant
🏨	Lodge
🚶	Trailhead
🚻	Restrooms
✦	Scenic Viewpoint
-----	Walking/Hiking Trails
······	Bicycle Path

Bryce Canyon Airport

TO HWY 89 AND ZION NAT'L PARK

Main Park Rd

Mossy Cave ✦

TROPIC CANYON

PINK CLIFFS

TO ESCALANTE →

5

Ruby's Inn 🪧 ⛺ 🍴

Fairyland Point ✦

Fairyland Loop Trail

Rim Trail

Visitor Center 🏚

North ⛺

Tower Bridge

Chinese Wall

General store

Sunrise Point ✦

Queens Garden Trail

Queens Garden

Bryce Canyon Lodge 🏨

Sunset Point 🪧

Thors Hammer

BRYCE AMPHITHEATER

Bryce Creek

The Cathedral

Sunset ⛺

Navajo Loop Trail

Peekaboo Loop Trail

TO RAINBOW POINT ↓

Inspiration Point ✦

Rim Trail

Wall of Windows

Rainbow Gate
Road closed from here to Rainbow Point during winter storms

Bryce Point ✦

Under-the-Rim Trail

0		1 mi
0		1 km

Paria View ✦

PINK CLIFFS

BRYCE CANYON NATIONAL PARK

EXPLORING BRYCE CANYON

Bryce Canyon consists of a scenic drive and a fanciful world of below-the-rim formations, all layered in the context of a peaceful park setting and one of the country's foremost windows into our planet's geologic history.

Visitors enter from the north just off a Utah Highway 12, a national scenic byway that crisscrosses the Grand Staircase–Escalante National Monument. With little buildup, the community of Bryce Canyon City (aka Ruby's Inn) greets you just outside the park boundary with a menagerie of hotels and tourist services. A few hundred yards beyond you enter the park, traveling 2 mi before encountering the entrance booth, visitor center, and primary park services.

On the 36-mi round-trip scenic drive, plan to make up to 13 stops to see the marvelous amphitheaters of Bryce from various perspectives. The Bryce Canyon Lodge area has a general store and the most prominent trailheads.

Although the park is open 365 days a year, many services inside the park close in early November due to the 200 inches of snow this plateau receives. As a result, throngs of visitors convene in the park's short summer. Come any other time of the year for fewer human encounters and plentiful tranquillity.

Remember that the plateau averages more than 8,000 feet above sea level, so persons with heart and/or breathing conditions should use common sense on hikes and other forms of physical exertions. Even physically fit, active adults can be victims of altitude sickness here, primarily headaches and lethargy in its typical mild form.

VISITOR CENTERS

Bryce Canyon Visitor Center. You can visit with park rangers, watch a video about Bryce Canyon, study exhibits, or shop for informative books, maps, and other materials at this spacious visitor center. First aid, emergency, and lost-and-found services are offered here, and rangers dole out backcountry permits. If you want coffee, head to the general store (summer only) or nearby Ruby's Inn. ⊠ *Main Park Rd., 1 mi south of park entrance* ☎ *435/834–5322* ⊕ *www.nps.gov/brca* ☉ *Oct.–June, daily 8–4:30; July–Sept., daily 8–8.*

Good Reads

Bryce Canyon Auto and Hiking Guide, by Tully Stoud, includes information on the geology and history of the area.

Supplement the free park map with *Trails Illustrated's Bryce Canyon Map,* which includes a detailed park hiking map, trail descriptions, and photographs.

To prepare kids ages 5–14 for a trip to the park, consider order-ing *Dangers in the Narrows,* which focuses on Bryce Canyon and Zion, it's one of a new se-ries of youth-oriented outdoor titles called Adventures with the Parkers.

Books are available at the visitor center or by contacting **Bryce Canyon Natural History Association** (☎ *435/834–4601* or *888/362–2642*).

SCENIC DRIVE

FodorśChoice Main Park Road. One of the delights of Bryce Canyon National Park is that much of the park's grandeur can be experienced from scenic overlooks along its main thoroughfare, which meanders 18 mi from the park entrance south to Rainbow Point. Allow two to three hours to travel the entire 36 mi round-trip. The road is open year-round but may be closed temporarily after heavy snowfalls to allow for clearing. Major overlooks are rarely more than a few steps' walk from the parking areas, and many let you see more than 100 mi on clear days. All overlooks lie east of the road. To keep things simple (and left turns to a minimum), proceed to the southern end of the park and stop at the overlooks on your northbound return. Trailers are not allowed beyond Sunset Campground. Day users may park trailers at the visitor center or other designated sites; check with park staff for parking options. RVs can drive throughout the park, but vehicles longer than 25 feet are not allowed at Paria View.

Scenic Byway 12. Irrespective of the contradiction of the Federal Highway Administration designating "scenic" roads, Highway 12 is a 124-mi winding journey through some of Utah's most rugged and dramatic landscape. A red rock tunnel (maximum clearance: 13 feet 6 inches) at Red Canyon (17 mi west of Bryce) serves as the unofficial entrance to this delightful drive. Also to the west, Tropic reservoir (the reservoir is west of Bryce, but the town is east of the park) is considered the best fishing in the area. To the east, it's 22 mi to Cannonville and one of four Grand

Festivals & Events

Bryce Canyon Half Marathon. Run from Ruby's Inn to Cannonville in July, including about 3 mi on Highway 12 inside Bryce Canyon National Park. Beat the heat with the 6 AM start. ☎800/444–6689.

Bryce Canyon Winter Fest. This February event at Ruby's Best Western Inn features cross-country ski races, snow-sculpting contests, and ski archery. ☎435/834–5341 or 866/866–6616.

Quilt Walk Festival. During the bitter winter of 1864, Panguitch residents were on the verge of starvation. A group of men from the settlement set out over the mountains to fetch provisions from the town of Parowan, 40 mi away. When they hit waist-deep snowdrifts, they were forced to abandon their oxen. Legend says the men, frustrated and ready to turn back, laid a quilt on the snow and knelt to pray. Soon they realized the quilt had kept them from sinking into the snow. Spreading quilts before them as they walked, leapfrog style, the men traveled to Parowan and back, returning with lifesaving provisions. Though it's held in July rather than in the dead of winter, the three-day event commemorates the event with quilting classes, a tour of Panguitch's pioneer homes, crafts shows, and a dinner-theater production in which the story is acted out. ☎435/676–8585 ⊕www.quilt walk.com.

Panguitch Pioneer Day Celebration. Celebrating the arrival of Brigham Young in Salt Lake City on July 24, 1847, Pioneer Day celebrations are common across the state. Panguitch features a rodeo, parade, historical programs, barbecue, children's races, dancing, and more. ☎435/676–8585 or 800/444–6689.

Panguitch Valley Balloon Rally. Every June, watch two dozen or more colorful hot-air balloons rise into the air at Panguitch and float over canyon country. ☎866/590–4134 ⊕www.panguitchvalleyballoon rally.com.

Utah Shakespearean Festival. This world-class festival in Cedar City features multiple stage productions as well as a free "green show," a nightly outdoor performance with jugglers, puppet shows, and actors dressed in Elizabethan period costume. Stop by to see the Adams Shakespearean Theatre, dedicated in 1977, whether there is a performance or not. The outdoor theater is patterned after the 16th-century Globe Theatre. The festival runs from June through October. ☎435/586–7880 or 800/752–9849 ⊕www.bard.org.

Staircase–Escalante National Monument visitor centers. Close by is Kodachrome Basin, a colorful moonlike landscape so photogenic it was said to be inspired by the creative minds of the filmmakers. Ten rough dirt-road miles beyond Koadachrome (go only during dry weather), lies one of Utah's most majestic and tallest arches, Grosvenor. Escalante Petrified Forest State Park is about 50 mi east of Bryce, with dinosaur and flora fossils.

HISTORIC SITES

Bryce Canyon Lodge. Gilbert Stanley Underwood designed this lodge, built in 1924, for the Union Pacific Railroad. The National Historic Landmark has been faithfully restored, right down to the lobby's huge limestone fireplace and log and wrought-iron chandelier, plus bark-covered hickory furniture made by the same company that created the originals. Inside the historic building are a restaurant and a gift shop, as well as plenty of information on park activities. Guests of the lodge stay in the numerous log cabins on the wooded grounds. (⇨*See Where to Eat & Stay in the Park.*) ⊠*Main Park Rd., 2 mi south of park entrance* ☎*435/834–5361.*

SCENIC STOPS

Agua Canyon. When you stop at this overlook in the southern section of the park, pick out among the hoodoos the formation known as the Hunter, which actually has a few small hardy trees growing on its cap. The play of light and colorful contrasts are especially noticeable here. ⊠*Main Park Rd., 12 mi south of park entrance.*

Bryce Point. Quite possibly the most panoramic vista in the park, follow a short trail to the lookout to get a view that extends nearly 360 degrees. Absorb views of the Black Mountains and Navajo Mountain, or follow the trailhead for the Under-the-Rim Trail to descend into the amphitheater to the Hat Shop. This cluster of top-heavy hoodoos has rocks poised precariously atop stone "columns"—as if some playful deity had planted them there for our amusement. Access the Peekaboo Loop Trail from here to see the **Wall of Windows.** (*Note:* The trail from Bryce Point to Peekaboo Loop Trail was closed in 2008 but is expected to be open in 2009.) ⊠*Main Park Rd., 5½ mi south of park entrance on Inspiration Point Rd.*

5

Fairyland Point. The bus doesn't stop here—and many visitors apparently follow suit. North of the visitor center (look for the sign marking the route off the main park road), this stop offers splendid views of Fairyland Amphitheater and its delicate, fanciful forms. The Sinking Ship and other formations stand before the grand backdrop of the Aquarius Plateau and distant Navajo Mountain. ⊠ *1 mi off Main Park Rd., 1 mi north of visitor center.*

Inspiration Point. Triple your pleasure at three different lookouts at Inspiration Point. Note the pure white limestone of the geologically youngest section of the Claron Formation, contrasted with the pink limestone, rich with iron below. Looking north toward Sunrise Point, see a massive cluster of hoodoos known as the "Silent city." This is a great spot to see the sunset. ⊠ *5½ mi south of park entrance on Inspiration Point Rd.*

Mossy Cave. Follow a short, well-marked trail alongside a tranquil brook (except during rare flash floods) and be rewarded with a cave, small waterfall, and some hoodoos. ⇨ *See Bryce Canyon Hikes & Activities for more information on the hike here.* ⊠ *Hwy. 12, 4 mi east of junction of Rte. 63 and Hwy. 12.*

Natural Bridge. There are hundreds, if not thousands, of arches in Utah, but this is the only one accessible by car in Bryce. The green pine forest visible through the bridge's 54-foot span provides great contrast to the reddish-yellow stone of the formation. Despite its name, this formation is actually an arch carved in the rock by rain and frost erosion; true natural bridges must be bored out by streams and rivers. ⊠ *Main Park Rd., 11 mi south of park entrance.*

Paria View. Gaze into the Paria River watershed below in a unique southwest-facing overlook. Far below you, hardy hikers on the Under-the-Rim Trail may be refilling their supplies at the lush, green Yellow Creek Meadow. Also, look for mule deer, elk, and pronghorn in the meadows near here—and peregrine falcons nesting or hunting along the cliffs. Skiers love this 3.5-mi cross-country loop in winter. ⊠ *7½ mi south of park entrance, off Bryce Point Rd..*

Rainbow and Yovimpa Points. Your best starting point for a half-day driving tour of Bryce Canyon, this double viewpoint is the highest and often coolest part of the park (more than 9,100 feet above sea level). Although Rainbow Point's

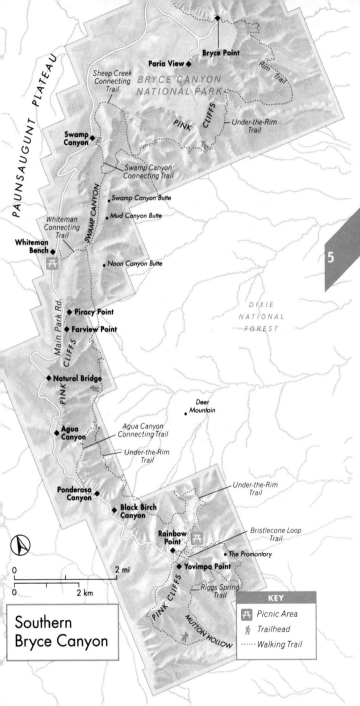

Bryce Point

Paria View

Sheep Creek Connecting Trail

BRYCE CANYON NATIONAL PARK

PAUNSAUGUNT PLATEAU

Rim Trail

PINK CLIFFS

Under-the-Rim Trail

Swamp Canyon

Swamp Canyon Connecting Trail

SWAMP CANYON

• *Swamp Canyon Butte*

• *Mud Canyon Butte*

Whiteman Connecting Trail

Whiteman Bench

• *Noon Canyon Butte*

DIXIE NATIONAL FOREST

5

Piracy Point

Main Park Rd.

Farview Point

PINK CLIFFS

Natural Bridge

Deer Mountain

Agua Canyon

Agua Canyon Connecting Trail

Under-the-Rim Trail

Ponderosa Canyon

Black Birch Canyon

Under-the-Rim Trail

Rainbow Point

Bristlecone Loop Trail

• *The Promontory*

Yovimpa Point

Riggs Spring Trail

PINK CLIFFS

MUTTON HOLLOW

0 — 2 mi
0 — 2 km

KEY
🏕 *Picnic Area*
🚶 *Trailhead*
····· *Walking Trail*

Southern Bryce Canyon

orientation allows a view north along the southern rim of the amphitheater and east into Grand Staircase–Escalante National Monument, the panorama from Yovimpa Point spreads out to the south and on a clear day you can see as far as 100 mi to Arizona. Yovimpa Point also has a shady and quiet picnic area with tables and restrooms. The Bristlecone Loop Trail connects the two viewpoints and leads through a grove of bristlecone pine trees. There are informative displays on flora, fauna, and geological history at Rainbow Point. ⊠*Main Park Rd., 18 mi south of park entrance.*

Sunrise Point. Named for its stunning views at dawn, this overlook is a popular stop for the summer crowds that come to Bryce Canyon and is the starting point for the Queen's Garden Trail and the Fairyland Loop Trail. You have to descend the Queen's Garden Trail to get a regal glimpse of **Queen Victoria,** a hoodoo that appears to sport a crown and glorious full skirt. The trail is popular and marked clearly, but moderately strenuous. ⊠*Main Park Rd., 2½ mi south of park entrance behind Bryce Canyon Lodge.*

Sunset Point. Bring your camera to watch the late-day sun paint its magic on the hoodoos here. You can only see **Thor's Hammer,** a delicate formation similar to a balanced rock, when you hike 521 feet down into the amphitheater on the Navajo Loop Trail. Also walk through Wall Street, a skyline of red rock that dwarfs you, and clusters of stubborn ponderosa pines that seem to grow out of rock. ⊠*Main Park Rd., 2½ mi south of park entrance near Bryce Canyon Lodge.*

Whiteman Bench. There are picnic tables here at this trailhead for the Swamp Canyon portion of the Under-the-Rim Trail. The views aren't spectacular even though you're atop the Pink Cliffs portion of the canyon. It's ideally located for a quick break during your start-and-stop drive. ⊠*Main Park Rd., 10 mi south of park entrance.*

Bryce Canyon Hikes & Activities

6

WORD OF MOUTH

"I'd try for sunrise at Bryce Point and hike Navajo Loop down and Queens Garden back up. Or [if you have] less time you can just do the Navajo Loop as a loop."

—Myer

By Steve
Pastorino

BRYCE CANYON AMPHITHEATER—a pleasant tree-lined plateau with North Campground, Bryce Lodge, Bryce General Store, and three canyon trailheads within walking distance—is the heart of any visit to this National Park. The hoodoos, tunnels, and chasms that sit just below the rim of this unique landscape are unlike anything in the world. Queen Victoria, Thor's Hammer, Wall Street, and the other formations are as fanciful as their names.

But move beyond the heart of the park to discover a magnificent drive to Yovimpa Point. If the elevation of 9,110 feet doesn't take your breath away, the panoramic view of up to 100 mi (on a clear day) may. Numerous pullouts on the drive (best stopped at on your northbound drive) reveal canyons, natural bridges, picnic areas, and more dramatic vistas.

Kids and adults alike will love the variety of ranger programs. Animal-seekers will find prairie dogs, mule deer, and pronghorns on the plateau, along with nearly 200 species of birds. With its limited traffic and speed limits, the main road attracts many cyclists who incorporate a ride in Bryce into their travels. And if you like to ride horses, few experiences compare with a trek down the Peekaboo Trail—it's a trip straight out of the Old West.

As you plan your activities, remember that the elevation cools Bryce days compared to some of its surrounding desert, but it also leaves you susceptible to intense sun during the day and freezing nights.

DAY HIKES

There's a pattern to hikes in Bryce—start at the rim, descend into the canyon, explore among the red rocks, then climb out. Because of the need to regain distance at the end of virtually every hiking trail in the park, all of these hikes will be moderately strenuous. To reach the hoodoos (caused by erosion, freezing, and thawing of the rim of a cliff), you'll have to endure steep and often uneven trails. Remember that bighorn sheep are more naturally inclined to this landscape than humans.

But if you want to get up close and personal with these wondrous formations, set aside at least a half-day for a hike. If you have time for just one trail, choose the Navajo Loop/Queen's Garden combination. With a little more time, pick

BEST HIKES & ACTIVITIES

■ **Wall Street:** Drop into the canyon from any rim trailhead for unforgettable landscapes and formations. Few inspire awe like the soaring rock towers of Wall Street.

■ **Natural Bridge:** The natural sandstone arch is one of the most recognized symbols of Utah, but many are in hard-to-reach locations. Enjoy this arch (it's technically not a bridge) just steps from your car at the trailhead with the same name.

■ **Ranger activities:** For a small park, Bryce has abundant entertaining and learning opportunities with park rangers. Enjoy a moonlight walk, canyon hike, geology talk, or astronomy session.

■ **Bristlecone Loop Trail:** Arrive at Rainbow & Yovimpa Point, and you'll have completed the first half of the Bryce Canyon scenic drive. This easy trail cuts under and around trees as old as 1,600 years and offers views as far as the Grand Canyon.

■ **Ski Utah:** With more than 20 mi of groomed trails, Bryce is a winter wonderland for skiers—and snowshoe enthusiasts as well. Snowmobiling and downhill skiing are available outside the park.

one of the outlying hikes: Fairyland Point, Riggs Springs, or the Hat Shop.

The base of the canyon is a 23-mi-long hike known as the Under-the-Rim Trail. If you're not planning on a backcountry hike through the park, you can get a taste for the forestlike canyon bottom via the Swamp Canyon or Whiteman Bench connecting trails; just remember that the climb out will be steep.

The uneven terrain calls for sturdy hiking boots. In summer, consider hiking in the morning to avoid the day's warmest temperatures and strongest sun. Keep in mind that if you're not used to exercising at elevation, you can fall victim to altitude sickness.

For trail maps, information, and ranger recommendations, stop at the park's visitor center. Bathrooms are at most trailheads but not down in the amphitheater.

HIKES TO LOOK OUT FOR

Short hikes (less than two hours): Navajo Trail, Queen's Garden, Mossy Cave, Rim Trail, Bristlecone Loop Trail.

Bryce Canyon's Shuttle System

The Bryce Canyon Shuttle is a voluntary service running between Ruby's Inn and Bryce Point (at the southern end of the Bryce Amphitheater). Significantly, it does *not* traverse the rest of the park—you must ride in a private vehicle (or bike or hike) to visit picnic grounds at Whiteman Bench or Rainbow Point; or any of the lookouts south of Bryce Point.

Shuttles operate approximately every 12 to 15 minutes from late May through the end of September. There's a loading area at Ruby's Inn just north of the park. The shuttle makes approximately a dozen stops during each loop. Although there's no fee for the shuttle itself, park entrance fee is required. Shuttle stops on each loop include:

(Southbound)
- Ruby's Inn
- Visitor Center
- Sunset Point
- Sunset Campground
- Bryce Point

(Northbound)
- Inspiration Point
- Sunset Campground
- Sunset Point
- Bryce Lodge
- Sunrise Point
- North Campground
- Visitor Center

Half-day hikes (up to five hours): Fairyland Loop Trail, Hat Shop Trail, Peekaboo Loop, Tower Bridge Trail.

Full-day hikes: Under-the-Rim Trail, Riggs Springs Loop Trail.

SPOTLIGHT HIKE: NAVAJO TRAIL / QUEEN'S GARDEN COMBINATION LOOP

Drop down into the exotic land of hoodoos in this prototypical walk through Bryce Canyon. Legendary formations come to life before you as you step under, around, between, and adjacent to one million years of geological history. This moderately strenuous combination of trails checks in at less than 3 mi, but will likely take you three hours. ✉ *Trailhead at Sunset and Sunrise points, Main Park Rd., 2 mi south of park entrance* ☞ *Moderate.*

0.0 MI: SUNSET POINT

The descent (including a series of switchbacks) will make you wish you'd brought rappelling gear—it's that tough. But the alternative, starting at Sunrise Point and hiking

NAVAJO TRAIL TIPS

■ Rangers recommend beginning the hike at Sunset Point and ending at Sunrise Point. The steepest sections are less than one-half mile—at the beginning and end of the trail.

■ Hardy kids will do okay on this trail, but little ones may tire and want to be carried up the final ascent, the point at which your legs and back are most fatigued. Take your time, bring plenty of "treats," and don't overextend your preschoolers' abilities.

■ If you doubt their ability to last 3-plus hours, choose Queen's Garden or Navajo Loop—not both.

■ The folks who visit national parks to see animals may be disappointed in Bryce, but it may explain why they take an excessive interest in the "domesticated" squirrels and chipmunks on this heavily touristed trail. Avoid the temptation to cater to the cute creatures.

out this way, is much tougher. Look for Thor's Hammer, but tread carefully.

0.3 MI: WALL STREET
Here, the popular moniker refers to the towers of rock that dwarf you as your legs recover from the shock of the steep descent. It's a dazzling introduction to the scale and wonder of Bryce Canyon.

0.8 MI: TRAIL JUNCTION
At the point where Navajo Trail and Queen's Garden meet, you find two premiums: shade and flat land. Relax and enjoy some of the nation's cleanest air. In the afternoons especially, the rest of the trail can bake under direct sun. If you're seeking more challenge, take the Peekaboo Loop from here for 3 more mi including the Wall of Windows and the Cathedral.

1.8 MI: QUEEN VICTORIA
Follow a short spur trail to see Queen Victoria. Now it takes imagination to look at a slowly eroding sandstone "sculpture" and give it a name, but here you can see her highness's head, crown, and gown easily. The Queen's Garden, for which the trail is named, delights the imagination with a multitude of formations.

Ever-Evolving Bryce

CLOSE UP

Bryce's enchanting formations are the result of millennia of erosion accelerated by baking-hot summer temperatures and icy high-altitude nights. Massive rock falls occur regularly—they are the natural effects of rain, frost, wind, and flowing water.

When 400 to 500 tons of rock crashed onto the Navajo Loop Trail on May 23, 2006, fortunately no one was close enough to get injured. An area 60 feet long and 15 feet wide near Wall Street was buried to a depth of 15 feet by debris. Some boulders were as large as cars. But such incidents are not that rare.

Bryce rangers report that in about 3 million years, the hoodoos will cease to exist as the canyon will have eroded all the way to the East Fork of the Sevier River.

2.9 MI: SUNRISE POINT

The ascent to Sunrise Point is much more subdued than the switchbacks at Sunset Point. Eventually, the dirt and limestone paths give way to paved trail, and the sounds of the canyon rim come alive. Savor the maze of impossibly balanced hoodoos, man-made tunnels, and inexplicably situated trees you've just walked among.

SPOTLIGHT HIKE: UNDER-THE-RIM TRAIL

At 23 mi in length and with significant up-and-down trekking that probably quadruples the 1,300-foot elevation difference from Rainbow Point to Bryce Point, this hike is not for everyone. For a remote, backcountry, solitude-filled sojourn, however, it can't be beat. A permit is required for an overnight stay in the backcountry: see a ranger at the visitor center before you depart. ⊠*Main Park Rd., 18 mi south of park entrance* ⌒*Difficult.*

0.0 MI: YOVIMPA POINT

Starting on the Bristlecone Loop trail, enjoy a half-mile of forested footsteps. Soon, though, you find yourself on sunny Ponderosa Ridge—walking a ridgeline with the Grand Canyon distantly to the south, and Bryce Point 23 mi to the north. Next thing you know, you've dropped to the base of the canyon and you're clambering over dry boulders in the river of rocks known as Birch Canyon.

3.9 MI: IRON SPRING

Water is a recurring theme in the backcountry here. Iron Spring is cited as a freshwater source, but in summer 2008 it trickled only about ½-inch deep and was extremely similar in color to the iron-soaked red cliffs above you and was not something you'd probably consider filtering and purifying. Maybe next year? In the meantime, there's a pretty little backcountry campsite a stone's throw from the trail.

10.8 MI: SWAMP CANYON

On a ridge at Agua Canyon (6.4 mi from Yovimpa Point), weary hikers can opt out and follow a ridgeline to the road (not that you'd have been able to park a car there). But if you stay with the hike you're rewarded with a trail that includes at least 3 mi under thick forest canopy, with scarcely a hoodoo or rock formation in sight. It might remind you of the Shenandoahs until you round a bend after passing the Swamp Canyon campsite (another nice one). Noon Canyon Butte (8,466 feet) rises up before you, with a pinnacle at its edge that seems to climb 1,000 feet in its own right. It's the first "take-your-breath-away" moment on this long hike.

13.0 MI: SHEEP CREEK CAMPGROUND TRAILHEAD

Sheep Creek and Yellow Creek are two of the most reliable sources of water in the Bryce backcountry. The Sheep Creek campsite (and water) are about 1 mi off the main trail. The site is not special, but the sound of gurgling water is heaven-sent if you've been carrying your own water for 13 mi. Be sure to bring a water purifier.

17.2 MI: YELLOW CREEK CAMPGROUND

This beautiful, shady campsite is adjacent to a year-round source of water. Choose a site a little back and up from the river, just in case rains bring flash flooding. The trail passed two moderate hills to arrive here, but you only notice the elevation change because you've been hiking for 10-plus hours.

20.4 MI: HAT SHOP

More than 20 mi (over at least two days for the average hikers) into your journey, the Hat Shop offers an up-close experience with some hoodoos that you otherwise don't get on the Under-the-Rim Trail. These playful characters feature boulders atop hoodoos on a lesser scale but still appear just as novel as Stonehenge or Easter Island. In this case, however, the attraction is 100% created by nature.

6

UNDER-THE-RIM TRAIL TIPS

■ The park's backcountry guide makes it pretty clear—but don't take this long walk to see hoodoos. The wall of the Claron Formation (the pinkish rock layer that has eroded to form hoodoos) is usually at least 1 mi away, abstract and not nearly as impressive as any of the hikes in Bryce Amphitheater.

■ The ascent from Hat Shop is tough, but the rim at Bryce Point is actually nearly 1,000 feet lower than Yovimpa Point. Yellow Creek was the lowest point in the park, at 6,620 feet, so you get the picture: lots of elevation gain/loss.

■ Freezing nights are recorded every month of the year in Bryce, sometimes on the heels of 80°F days. Bring all sorts of layers.

■ Backcountry perils include flash floods, lightning strikes, dehydration, hypothermia, cougars, black bears (extremely rare), rattlesnakes, and getting lost. This is not a very technical hike, but it doesn't diminish the dangers. Be prepared.

23.0 MI: BRYCE POINT

Following the Hat Shop, prepare for a churning ascent to the rim: 1,000 feet in elevation gain in less than 1½ mi.

OTHER TRAILS

☼ **Bristlecone Loop Trail.** Hike through dense spruce and fir forest to exposed cliffs, where ancient bristlecone pines somehow manage to survive the elements; some of the trees here are more than 1,600 years old. You might see yellow-bellied marmots and blue grouse, critters not found at lower elevations in the park. The popular 1-mi trail takes less than an hour to hike. ⊠*Rainbow Point, Main Park Rd., 18 mi south of park entrance* ⚲*Easy.*

Fairyland Loop Trail. Hike into whimsical Fairyland Canyon on this strenuous, sparsely visited 8-mi trail. It winds around hoodoos, across trickles of water, and finally to a natural window in the rock at Tower Bridge, 1½ mi from Sunrise Point and 4 mi from Fairyland Point. The pink-and-white badlands and hoodoos surround you the whole way. Allow four to five hours round-trip. You can pick up the loop at Fairyland Point, or at Sunrise Point, 1 mi farther south. ⊠*Fairyland Point, 1 mi off Main Park Rd., 1 mi south of park entrance* ⚲*Difficult.*

Bryce's Native American History

According to Paiute legend, the hoodoos are Legend People, predecessors who were turned to stone by coyotes, some still with paint on their faces.

Human history in Bryce Canyon dates back some 2,000 years to the Ancestral Puebloans, also known as Anasazi. The Fremont people are believed to have lived in the area in the 1200s, followed by the Paiute. According to Greer Chesher's *Bryce Canyon*, the Paiutes depended on springs "in and around Bryce, like *piki-pa* below Yovimpa Point, which may be what we know today as Riggs Spring." In summer, the Fremont and Paiute cultures would have been attracted by the Bryce rim's pine nuts, sego lily roots, and animals for nourishment.

The arrival of Mormon settlers in the 19th century, however, soon heralded the end of the Paiute relationship with the lands in and around Bryce.

Hat Shop Trail. Once you reach the end of this hike, you'll understand how the trail got its name. Hard gray caps balance precariously atop narrow pedestals of softer, rust-color rock. Allow three to four hours to travel this 4-mi round-trip trail. This is a difficult trail since the hike out is all uphill and steep. ⊠*Bryce Point, 2 mi off Main Park Rd., 5½ mi south of park entrance* ☞*Difficult.*

☾ **Mossy Cave Trail.** This short hike (0.8 mi) has a little bit of everything you might be looking for in Bryce: the sound of rushing water, a small waterfall, a cave, and hoodoos. The trailhead is on Highway 12, north and east of the main entrance. Ironically, the stream along which you hike isn't really a river—it's an irrigation ditch dug almost 100 years ago by Tropic farmers looking to divert water from the Sevier River for agriculture. Since the dig predates the park, the water right-of-way belongs to the farmers. ⊠*Hwy. 12, 4 mi east of junction with Rte. 63 (or 7 mi northeast of park entrance)* ☞*Easy.*

Navajo Loop Trail. A steep descent via a series of switch-backs leads to Wall Street, a narrow canyon with high rock walls and towering fir trees. The northern end of the trail brings Thor's Hammer into view. Allow one to two hours on this 1½-mi trail. Connect this hike with Queen's Garden Loop for an enjoyable half-day hike (but bring water). ⊠*Sunset Point, Main Park Rd., 2 mi south of park entrance* ☞*Moderate.*

6

Peekaboo Loop. For a good workout, hike this steep trail past the Wall of Windows and the Three Wise Men. Horses use this trail in spring, summer, and fall and have the right-of-way. The longer version of the trail begins at Bryce Point, but you can also join the trail at Sunrise or Sunset Point. Allow four hours to hike the 7-mi loop, three hours for the 5-mi loop. ⊠ *Bryce Point, 2 mi off Main Park Rd., 5½ mi south of park entrance* ☞ *Difficult.*

Queen's Garden. This hike is the easiest into the amphitheater and therefore the most crowded. The descent is "only" 320 feet and is fairly gradual. Enjoy countless hoodoos and rock formations, and the trail's namesake Queen Victoria icon off a spur trail at the turnaround point. Allow two to three hours to hike the 2 mi down and back. ⊠ *Sunrise Point, Main Park Rd., 2 mi south of park entrance* ☞ *Easy.*

Riggs Spring Loop Trail. One of the park's more rigorous day hikes, or a relaxed overnighter, this 9-mi trail between Yovimpa and Rainbow points takes about four to five hours to hike. The trail starts at the park's highest point (9,115 feet above sea level) and descends to Riggs Springs (7,443 feet) before climbing back out again. The trail is well-marked, and the views spectacular, but the ascent is challenging due to the altitude. Riggs Springs is one of the few reliable water sources in the backcountry, but treat the water before drinking it. ⊠ *Yovimpa and Rainbow points, Main Park Rd., 18 mi south of park entrance* ☞ *Difficult.*

Rim Trail. An ideal way to launch or wrap up your day, this 1-mi trail connects Sunrise and Sunset points. Take your time strolling. Evening may be the best time for photos as much of the rim looks out to the east. Listen for songbirds, look for a silent swooping owl, and watch the sun's last rays dance on the hoodoos. More ambitious walkers will enjoy the long, flat 5.2-mi walk between Bryce Point and Fairyland Point. ⊠ *Sunrise and Sunset points, Main Park Rd., 2 mi south of park entrance* ☞ *Easy.*

Tower Bridge. This short hike on the Fairyland Loop Trail takes you to a natural bridge deep in the amphitheater. Walk through pink and white "badlands," with hoodoos all around, on this 3-mi trip (not a loop) that takes two to three hours. The 950-foot elevation change may scare some casual hikers away, but the positive side is that you can have more quiet and solitude than on more popular park trails. ⊠ *Sunrise Point, 1 mi off main park road, south of park entrance* ☞ *Moderate.*

CLOSE UP

Bryce Canyon Geology

It's hard to imagine a prehistoric freshwater lake covering much of Utah and the southwest, but geologists are certain of its former presence. More than 65 million years ago, a network of rivers carried a variety of sediments including iron (yellow and red) and manganese (pink and violet), combining with calcium carbonate (cream) to create Bryce's signature colored limestone. This 1,300-foot deep layer is known as the Claron Formation.

Less than 15 million years ago, an uplift in the Colorado Plateau created a series of smaller plateaus including the Paunsaugunt (the "rim" of Bryce Canyon) and Tables Cliffs (the stunning formation visible as you look east). Water then shaped Bryce's accelerated erosion, not by its volume (a mere 18 inches of precipitation annually) but by the freezing and thawing that takes place more than 200 nights per year.

Finally, streams of water trickle down Bryce's rim forming gullies, cutting deep, narrow channels (called fins) into walls of rock. The fins develop windows, which grow larger (like Natural Bridge) until the roof collapses creating a hoodoo.

6

SUMMER SPORTS & ACTIVITIES

AIR TOURS

Bryce Canyon Airlines & Helicopters (☎*435/834–5341* ◉*www. rubysinn.com/bryce-canyon-airlines.html*) offers an aerial view of Bryce Canyon National Park by helicopter piloted by professional pilots and guides. Flights depart from Ruby's Inn Heliport. You can swoop over the amphitheater for anywhere from 15 minutes to more than an hour and cost from $55 per person for a short flight to $225 per person for a longer flight. Small airplane tours and charter services are also available.

BICYCLING

Riding inside Bryce Canyon will not be the easiest 40 mi in your life (20 mi each way from Ruby's Inn to Rainbow Point), but it certainly is a great workout. It's not traffic-free, either, but if you hit the road at dawn you'll have a lot of road to yourself. Officially, the elevation gain from north to south is only about 1,200 feet, but when you're going from 7,890 feet (above sea level) to 9,110 feet, your body is really going to feel it. There are some radical curving descents along the way, which only lead to more climbing . . . and more climbing. For an easier go, have a friend drive you to Rainbow Point, and bike back to the entrance one-way.

Mountain bike or hybrid riders should pay heed to the Great Western Trail, which bisects Route 63 between Ruby's Inn and the Fairyland Point turnout. Open to bikes, four-wheelers, horses, and (in winter) snowmobiles, the trail can be followed for up to about 400 mi across Utah alone. Someday, the trail is envisioned to connect Mexico and Canada.

Ruby's Inn Mountain Bike Rentals (⊠*Best Western Ruby's Inn, 1000 South Hwy. 63, Bryce Canyon City* ☎*435/834–5232* ⊕*www.rubysinn.com/biking.html*) rents mountain bikes for half-day or full-day excursions. The hotel can also recommend single-track trails in the surrounding region (bikes are not allowed off-road in the park.

BIRD-WATCHING

More than 170 bird species have been identified in Bryce. Violet green swallows and white-throated swifts are common, as are Steller's jays, American coots, Rufous hummingbirds, and mountain bluebirds. Lucky bird-watchers will see golden eagles floating across the skies above the pink rocks of the amphitheater. The best time in the park for avian variety is from May through July.

HORSEBACK RIDING

Few activities conjure up the Old West like riding a horse, and Bryce Canyon offers plenty of opportunities to see the sights from the saddle. Many of the park's hiking trails were first formed beneath the hooves of cattle wranglers, and their modern-day counterparts now guide tourists over these and other trails. Canyon Trail Rides is the only outfitter with permission to conduct rides in the park. Several area outfitters offer rides in the surrounding Dixie National Forest and Grand Staircase–Escalante National Monument. Minimum rider age and maximum rider weight vary according to the chosen ride (anywhere from a half hour to a full day or more in length), but typically those under the age of 7 and over the weight of 230 pounds are prohibited.

CLOSE UP

Star Gazers!

Bryce's clear, thin air and high-altitude location make it one of the darkest spots in North America. According to rangers, nearly 7,500 stars are visible to the unaided eye here (compared with 2,500 in a typical moonless small-town setting).

Venus rises early in the night, often followed by Vega and Arcturus. On cloudless nights, you will soon see the Milky Way, currently visible to less than 50% of the Northern hemisphere.

As a result, astronomy programs are common in summer—with ranger-led programs held most Wednesdays and Fridays between May and September. Check *The Hoodoo* newspaper for full moon hikes in summer as well, but dress warmly since nighttime temperatures approach freezing during much of the year.

Canyon Trail Rides (✉ *Bryce Canyon Lodge, Main Park Rd., about 2 mi south of park entrance* ☎ *435/679–8665*) is the only outfitter with permission to conduct trail rides in the park itself. You'll descend on horse- or muleback to the floor of the Bryce Canyon amphitheater. Most who take this expedition have no riding experience, so don't hesitate to join in. A two-hour ride ambles along the amphitheater floor to the Fairy Castle before returning to Sunrise Point. The half-day expedition follows Peekaboo Trail, winds past the Fairy Castle and the Alligator, and passes the Wall of Windows before returning to Sunrise Point. To reserve a trail ride, call or stop by their desk in the lodge.

Ruby's Red Canyon Horseback Rides (✉ *1000 S. Hwy. 63* ☎ *866/782–0002* ⊕ *www.horserides.net*), across the street from the hotel, offers a variety of tours outside the park in summer and winter. As indicated by their name, a favorite destination is Red Canyon, a miniature version of Bryce with red rocks and hoodoos. Ruby's tours will show you where outlaw Butch Cassidy used to ride. Rides last from a half hour to all day.

WINTER SPORTS

Unlike Utah's other national parks, Bryce Canyon usually receives plenty of snow, making it a popular cross-country ski area. The park's 2½-mi Fairyland Ski Loop is marked but not groomed, as is the 5-mi Paria Loop, which runs through ponderosa forests into long, open meadows. In addition to skiing, snowshoeing is popular, with rangers leading snowshoe hikes weekly in winter if there's enough snow.

Best Western Ruby's Inn (⊠*Rte. 63, 1 mi north of park entrance* ☎*435/834–5341* ⊕*www.rubysinn.com*) rents skis and other equipment during the winter snow season to get you to the rim of Bryce Canyon, which is about a mile from the hotel. There are 20 mi of groomed trails outside the park, and plenty of places to explore inside the park as well. Snowshoes are also available. Ask about snowmobiling excursions in the national forest outside of the park.

EXPLORING THE BACKCOUNTRY

One of the smallest National Parks by area, Bryce Canyon does not have the extended backcountry of places like Grand Canyon and Zion. Riggs Springs Loop has backcountry campsites, but since it's a 9-mi hike, many prefer to do it in one day.

The only other backcountry hiking and camping is on the 23-mi Under-the-Rim Trail (⇨*Day Hikes, above*). Situated almost entirely at the base of canyon, this might be the only place where hikers might get lost in the woods and encounter bears and mountain lions. Allow at least two days to hike the length of the trail in either direction. For a shorter version, drop down to the trail at any of four connecting trails along the park road. Unless you want to walk along the park road, you'll need to arrange a pick-up or drop-off, as the park shuttle service does not cover the full length of the park.

EDUCATIONAL PROGRAMS

PROGRAMS & TOURS

Bryce Canyon Scenic Tours. Enjoy a scenic two-hour tour of Bryce Canyon with knowledgeable guides who describe the area's history, geology, and flora and fauna. Choose from a sunrise tour, sunset tour, or general tour of the park. Specialized or private tours can also be arranged. Tours prices start at $26. ☎ *435/834–5351 or 866/834–0043.*

Campfire and Auditorium Programs. Bryce Canyon's natural diversity is brought to life by rangers and other park staff in the park's two campgrounds or at Bryce Canyon

CLOSE UP

Bryce Canyon Backcountry Trips

If you head into Bryce's backcountry, remember that a permit is required for camping. Also, rangers remind you to remember several important safety tips:

■ Even short paths and trails can be steep, narrow, and slippery; wear shoes with good traction.

■ Bryce temperatures can soar into the mid-90s F in summer, so drink plenty of water.

■ Subfreezing nights are recorded nearly every month of every year, so bring extra layers if your hike may keep you out past dusk.

■ Park altitudes climb to 9,110 feet; mild exertion at this altitude may leave you feeling light-headed and nauseated. You're also more susceptible to sunburn in the high, thin air here.

■ Do not feed wildlife. Speaking of animals, leave yours at home: pets are not permitted on any Bryce trail.

■ Take out everything you bring; leave behind everything you find.

6

Lodge. Lectures, slide programs, and audience participation introduce you to geology, astronomy, wildlife, history, and many other topics related to Bryce Canyon and the West. The lodge and Sunset campground are wheelchair-accessible; North Campground campfire circle is not. ☎*435/834–5322.*

High Plateau Institute. In 2004 Bryce Canyon launched a series of educational programs in conjunction with the Bryce Canyon Natural History Association. The institute presents many science-based learning opportunities in and around the park. ☎ *435/834–4603.*

HIGH PLATEAU INSTITUTE. A collaboration among the Bryce Canyon Natural History Association, Bryce Canyon National Park, and local businesses, as well as civic and academic institutions, the High Plateau Institute (HPI) offers opportunities for science- and culture-based learning. Year-round educational programs may cover topics such as geology, astronomy, plants, wildlife, ranching, or cowboy poetry. Kids' programs and special events also dot the calendar. The HPI is near Sunrise Point adjacent to the store.

RANGER PROGRAMS

The base of operations for all ranger activities is the visitor center, 4½ mi south of the intersection of Highway 12 and Highway 63. Admission to all programs is free, but meeting times and locations vary. Stop by the visitor center to get a list of what's on for the day(s) of your visit.

Astronomy Programs. Bryce Canyon is proud of some of the darkest skies in America, so it's no surprise the park has a NASA Solar System Ambassador in residence and twice-weekly stargazing programs throughout the summer. These are held Wednesday and Friday, weather permitting, and guests are able to view the skies through telescopes.

☾ **Canyon Hike.** Take an early-morning walk among the hoodoos of Queen's Garden or Navajo Loop Trail. A ranger points out the formations and explains some of the amphitheater's features as you go. The hike is about 2 mi long and takes two to three hours to complete. In winter (weather conditions permitting), don snowshoes for a ranger hike along the rim instead.

Geology Talk. Rangers relate the geologic story of Bryce Canyon in 30-minute sessions held twice a day in summer at Sunset Point, daily in late spring and early fall and occasionally in winter as well.

☾ **Junior Ranger Program.** Children ages 6 to 12 are encouraged sign up at the park visitor center for a fun and interactive program. Junior Rangers are required to attend a ranger activity and complete a series of exercises (depending on age) from a printed program guide. On completion of the program, rangers "swear in" their youth counterparts.

Moonlight Hike. Offered about twice a month near full moons, these hikes may focus on stars, hoodoos, nocturnal animals, or all of the above. Dress warmly—at this altitude, temperatures drop below freezing at least once every month of the year. Reservations are accepted (and are required during busy months), so inquire at the visitor center for schedules and reservations. Hikes are 1.5 to 2 mi and last about two hours.

☾ **Rim Walk.** This easy stroll is perfect for young or old family members who can't make it up and down Bryce's steep trails. As with most ranger programs, this 1-mi walk may be the most informative 60 to 90 minutes you spend in the park. Rangers are well-prepared, courteous, and friendly—and most go out of their way to attend walkers of all ages.

Utah Prairie Dog

CLOSE UP

Bryce Canyon National Park re-introduced the Utah prairie dog (*Cynomys parvidens*) in park meadows during the 1970s and 1980s. Numbering approximately 200 in Bryce today (and less than 5,000 across the southwest portion of the state), the Utah prairie dog has been listed as a "threatened species" under the Endangered Species Act since 1973. Bryce is the only National Park Service unit where the Utah prairie dog is found.

These rodents (they're not canines—but you knew that, right?) live in underground social colonies with multiple chambers where the animals raise their young, store food, and hibernate. If you see them skittering about park meadows, please don't approach them and drive carefully as they do cross park roads.

SHOPPING

Other than the kitschy Ruby's Inn, there are few options for groceries and general merchandise in the immediate vicinity of Bryce Canyon. There's a small grocery store in Tropic. Otherwise, Cedar City and Panguitch are your best options.

Bryce Canyon Lodge Gift Shop (⊠*Bryce Canyon Lodge, off main park road about 2 mi south of park entrance* ☎435/834–5361) carries Native American and Southwestern crafts, T-shirts, dolls, books, souvenirs, and sundries; however, it's closed from November through March.

Bryce Canyon Pines General Store (⊠*About ½ mi off main park road, 2 mi south of park entrance* ☎800/892–7923) has groceries, T-shirts, hats, books, film, postcards, and camping items that you might have left behind, as well as snacks, drinks, juices, and quick meals at this multipurpose facility at Sunrise Point. Picnic tables under pine trees offer a shady break. It's closed from mid-November to March.

Bryce Visitor Center (⊠*About 1 mi south of park entrance* ☎435/834–4601 or 888/362–2642) contains a bookstore operated by the Bryce Canyon National History Association; the store also sells maps, trail guides, videos, and postcards.

Old Bryce Town Shops (⊠*Across street from Ruby's Inn, Rte. 63, north of park entrance* ☎435/834–5355), owned by Ruby's Inn but across the street, include a gem shop, ice-cream parlor, leather goods, souvenirs, and holiday decorations. The shops are closed from October through April.

Ruby's General Store (⊠*Rte. 63, north of park* ☎*435/834–5341*) has been a souvenir heaven and an integral part of the Bryce Canyon experience for decades. This large, lively store is open year-round and is packed with everything imaginable emblazoned with the park's name, from thimbles to sweatshirts. Native American arts and crafts, Western wear, camping gear, groceries, and sundries are plentiful. There's a large selection of children's toys and trinkets.

Where to Eat & Stay in Bryce Canyon

INCLUDING TROPIC

WORD OF MOUTH

"In Bryce . . . Canyon I'd recommend staying in the park as the alternative accommodation is further out and you get a great atmosphere in the [park] before and after the main tourist rush."
—planning_ahead

By Steve
Pastorino

GOOD PLANNING IS KEY TO GETTING THE BEST HOTEL ROOMS and having at least one outstanding meal on a trip to Bryce Canyon. As it's an hour from any interstate and several more from an airport of any significance, the canyon is well off the beaten path. There's not a huge variety of accommodations, and some are considerably more rustic than others. But all of them—as well as the area's campgrounds—fill up fast in summer. Book ahead to avoid being locked out of even the most basic of places close to the park.

When it comes to nourishment, meat-and-potatoes home-style cooking reigns. Menus are unimaginative, fresh vegetables are rare, and healthful options are sparse in the dozen or so eateries on Highway 12, from Route 89 to Tropic. That said, there are a few area gems, and you can always arrange to access Bryce via Cedar City, Saint George, Escalante, or Salt Lake City, where you're sure to find more sophisticated fare.

WHERE TO EAT

You come to Bryce for hoodoos, not haute cuisine. It's a good thing as, from Tropic to Bryce to Panguitch to Hatch, you'll be hard-pressed to find a memorable restaurant.

That being said, Bryce Canyon Lodge serves above-average cuisine and has an authentic park lodge atmosphere. If you like fruit, be on the lookout for locally grown produce and fresh-baked pies. Locals rave about the Mexican food at Hatch's Café Adobe (it's 13 mi west on Highway 12 and 8 mi south on Highway 89; see Chapter 8, What's Nearby).

What's more, a frequently changing roster of chefs and eateries means you just might stumble upon a real find. (If you do, be sure to share it with us on Fodors.com.)

Note that the convenience stores in the immediate vicinity of the park and grocery stores in Tropic, Bryce Canyon City (Ruby's Inn), and Panguitch are the only outposts for food and sundries. Plan accordingly.

WHAT IT COSTS				
¢	$	$$	$$$	$$$$
under $8	$8–$12	$13–$20	$21–$30	over $30

Restaurant prices are per person for a main course at dinner and do not include any service charges or taxes.

IN THE PARK

$$–$$$ ✕**Bryce Canyon Lodge.** *American.* To its credit, concessionaire Xanterra has tried to develop the menus and improve the quality of the food—without sending prices into orbit—at the national park lodges it operates. Bryce Canyon Lodge is no exception. This rustic old lodge is the only place to dine within the park. Come for at least one meal surrounded by towering pines outside and historic photographs within. Steaks, chops, and fish might be prepared with a coriander-cornmeal crust, a cherry glaze, or a Thai chili sauce. Outstanding vegetarian options include gnocchi, Portobello steak, and vegetable strudel. Choose from nearly two dozen wines on a list topped by a $55 bottle of Coppola Syrah from Napa, California. Reservations are essential at dinner. *About 2 mi south of park entrance* ☎*435/834–5361* ⊕*www.brycecanyonlodge.com* ⟨*Reservations essential* ═*AE, D, DC, MC, V* ⊙*Closed Nov.–Mar.*

7

OUTSIDE THE PARK

$$ ✕**Bryce Canyon Pines Resort.** *American.* A banner at this restaurant-motel complex about 6 mi west of Bryce Canyon City advertises homemade soups and pies. Do expect pine-paneled walls, rodeo photos, a fireplace, antiques, and filling comfort food. Don't expect fresh vegetables or many other healthful options. If you stop to sample the desserts, pies made with such locally grown fruits as raspberry and apple are your best bets, though there are usually a dozen varieties, including unique offerings like banana-blueberry-cream. Entrées include steaks, burgers, and hot and cold sandwiches. There's a limited beer and wine list and a kids' menu. *Mile Marker 10, Hwy. 12* ☎*435/834–5330* ⊕*www.brycecanyonmotel.com* ═*MC, V* ⊙*Closed Nov.–Mar.*

$–$$ ✕**Clarke's Restaurant.** *American.* When it comes to humble Tropic's handful of restaurants, Clarke's is the pick of the litter. Adjacent to Bryce Valley Inn, an ice-cream shop, and the town's general store, its location couldn't be more central. Clarke's serves up burgers, steaks, and other hearty dishes—just what you'd expect of true meat-and-potatoes place with a faux-brick walls and a Western-theme decor. Sidle up to a booth with the kids, or order drinks from the bar. In summer you can also eat on the patio. ✉ *199 N. Main St. , Tropic* ☎*435/838–3199* ▭*MC, V* ⊘*Closed Nov.–Mar.*

$–$$ ✕**Fosters Family Steakhouse.** *Steak.* Fosters is a clean, relatively quiet steak house about 2 mi west of Bryce Canyon City and the junction of Route 63. A stone fireplace and picture windows lend a charm that's only slightly diminished by the dated, red faux-leather booths and walnut-stained country furnishings. Prices for beef and basic chicken and seafood dishes are comparable to those at other area restaurants. Beer is the only alcohol served. *1150 Hwy. 12* ⊕*435/834–5227* ⊕*www.fostersmotel.com* ▭*AE, D, MC, V* ⊘*Closed Mon.–Thurs. in Jan.*

$$ **Mexican & American Restaurant.** *Southwestern.* Despite erratic service and an ambitious Southwestern menu, this restaurant in the Bryce Canyon Resort has potential. The Western-theme dining room has quiet alcoves, and it's sure to be the only place where you can find ceviche on the list of starters. Entrées include such dishes as *sopes* (a traditional Mexican tortilla topped with beans, cheese, salsa, and other toppings) and shrimp-stuffed tilapia. In an attempt to cater to every Bryce visitor, there's a kids' menu as well as a beer list that suggests this is the place to go drinking on a Friday night. Try a draft from Squatters, Wasatch, or Zion Canyon—all prominent Utah craft brewers. *139 W. Hwy. 12* ☎*435/834–5351* ⊕*www.brycecanyonresort.com* ▭*AE, D, MC, V*

PICNIC AREAS

North Campground. This area amid ponderosa pines has picnic tables and grills. ✉ *About ¼ mi south of Bryce Canyon National Park Visitor Center.*

Yovimpa Point. At the southern end of the park, this shady, quiet spot looks out onto the 100-mi vistas from the rim. There are tables and restrooms. ✉*18 mi south of Bryce Canyon National Park entrance.*

WHERE TO STAY

For many who explore the west's national parks, staying in a park lodge is the only way to go. Bryce Canyon Lodge may not have as much charm or history as other such lodges, but it's the best option here, hands-down, in terms of price, location, food, and character.

The park's gateway community, Bryce Canyon City, has Ruby's Inn and two other hotels. Ruby's is a monstrosity, with nearly 400 rooms and a theme-park feel that overwhelms its historical importance (for years it was literally the only place to stay).

Southwestern Utah is steeped in pioneer heritage, and many older homes are also bed-and-breakfasts. There are also a number of motels in small towns and unincorporated areas near the park. Bryce Canyon Pines Resort and Bryce Canyon Resort (don't confuse the two) are among them.

Camping is a great option, though freezing nights are possible at any time of the year given the elevation (which ranges from 6,600 in the amphitheater to nearly 8,000 feet at the park's entrance). If you're stocking up for your campsite or kitchenette, hit the groceries in Panguitch or Cedar City for the best variety and prices.

Reserve rooms and campsites ahead for the summer high season. If you're willing to stay upward of an hour away from the park, you may be able to get same-day reservations. The properties may have fewer amenities but also lower rates. Panguitch has some particularly good options for budget and last-minute travelers (⇨*see Chapter 8, What's Nearby*).

WHAT IT COSTS				
¢	$	$$	$$$	$$$$
under $70	$70–$120	$121–$175	$176–$250	over $250

Hotel prices are for a double room in high season and do not include taxes, service charges, or resort fees.

IN THE PARK

★ Fodor'sChoice ⊞**Bryce Canyon Lodge.** A few yards from the
$$$ amphitheater's rim and trailheads is this rugged stone-and-
wood lodge. There's a variety of guest quarters: suites on
the lodge's second level, rooms with balconies or porches
in separate motel-style buildings, and cozy pole-pine cabins,
some with cathedral ceilings and gas fireplaces. Rooms
here are hard to come by, so call several months ahead.
Dinner reservations are essential at the restaurant. You can
arrange horseback rides into the park's interior. **Pros:** in-
park location with easy access to rim for viewing sunrises
and sunsets, good restaurant, good for families. **Cons:** few
amenities, closed in winter. ✉*Bryce Canyon National Park,
Box 640079* ☎ *435/834–8700 or 888/297–2757* ⊕ *www.
brycecanyonlodge.com* ⇨*70 rooms, 3 suites, 40 cabins*
⌂*In-room: no a/c, no TV. In-hotel: restaurant, no-smoking
rooms, no elevator* ⊟*AE, D, DC, MC, V* ⊘*Closed
Nov.–Mar.*

OUTSIDE THE PARK

$$ ⊞**Best Western Ruby's Inn.** In 2007 Ruby's became incorpo-
rated as Utah's 244th official town—which gives you an
idea how big this enterprise is. It's just north of the entrance
to Bryce Canyon National Park, but it's more akin to a
theme park than a typical gateway community. Virtually
everything you can think of is available in this complex: a
hotel, campground, large general store, gas station, ice-
cream parlor, gift shop, liquor store, and several restaurants.
Because wings were added to the hotel gradually through
the years, rooms vary in age. All are comfortable and attractive with gem-tone, quilt-patterned bedspreads contrasted
against maple furnishings. The lobby of rough-hewn log
beams and poles sets a Southwestern mood. Ruby's can
arrange almost any local activity. Choose from an on-site
evening rodeo (Wednesday through Saturday from late
May to September), scenic flights, snow sports in the winter,
guided hiking and horseback riding, ATV tours, and mountain bike rentals. **Pros:** size means rooms might be available
on short notice, family friendly, and everything imaginable
on-site. **Cons:** not very peaceful, nothing is cheap. ✉*1000
S. Hwy. 63, Bryce Canyon City* ☎ *435/834–5341 or
866/866–6616* ⊕ *www.rubysinn.com* ⇨*383 rooms, 2
suites* ⌂*In-room: dial-up. In-hotel: 2 restaurants, 2 pools,
bicycles, laundry facilities* ⊟ *AE, D, DC, MC, V.*

$–$$ 🏨**Bryce Canyon Pines Resort.** Don't let the "resort" in the name fool you: this is a no-surprises motel. It's a quiet and pleasant place in the woods 6 mi northwest of the entrance to Bryce Canyon National Park. Motel units and cabins, most with adjacent parking, house rooms and suites. Many accommodations have excellent mountain and valley views. Ask for the newer and/or updated rooms. There's also a campground and a home-style restaurant on the premises. **Pros:** good value, above-average, on-site restaurant, hospitable family owners. **Cons:** on a busy two-lane rural road but feels a little "middle of nowhere." ✉ *Hwy. 12, Bryce* ☎ *435/834–5330 or 800/892–7923* ⊕ *www.brycecanyon motel.com* ⏍*51 rooms* ⚬*In-hotel: restaurant, pool, no elevator* ▭ *AE, D, DC, MC, V.*

$$–$$$ 🏨**Bryce Canyon Resort.** It's a rustic lodge 3 mi north of the Bryce Canyon National Park entrance and just across the way from the local airport. Many of the rooms have been updated with fresh paint, carpet, and new bathrooms; some bathrooms have two sinks—a nice touch. Newer cabins and cottages offer a tad more privacy than their older counterparts. **Pros:** convenient location, on-site ATV rental. **Cons:** no landscaping, restaurant's food quality and service are erratic. ✉ *139 W. Hwy. 12, Bryce* ☎ *435/834–5256 or 800/834–0043* ⊕ *www.brycecanyonresort.com* ⏍*54 rooms, 2 suites, 14 cabins* ⚬*In-room: dial-up. In-hotel: restaurant, pool, laundry facilities, some pets allowed, no elevator* ▭ *AE, D, MC, V.*

$ 🏨**Bryce Valley Inn.** Rest your head in this down-to-earth motel with the timber exterior in the tiny town of Tropic. Updated rooms feature faux-leather sofas and traditional table lamps. It's hard to tell where the inn, the adjacent restaurant, ice-cream shop, and general store begin and end, but all are worth a stroll before Tropic rolls up the sidewalks. The on-site gift shop sells Native American crafts. **Pros:** price is right, Tropic is a friendly little town. **Cons:** no real character, no frills. ✉ *199 N. Main St., Tropic* ☎ *435/679–8811 or 800/442–1890* ⊕ *www.brycevalleyinn.com* ⏍*65 rooms* ⚬*In-hotel: restaurant, laundry facilities, no-smoking rooms, some pets allowed* ▭ *AE, D, MC, V.*

$ 🏨**Bryce View Lodge.** This lodge next to the park entrance is owned by the Syrett family, the same people who own Ruby's Inn across the street. Rates at Bryce View are more reasonable than at Ruby's, and you have access to all the same amenities and services—including the pools, horseback riding, shops, and more. Rooms are on the small side, but are comfortable. **Pros:** reasonable room rates, access to lots of facilities. **Cons:** construction all around will likely lead to congestion in 2009. ⊠*Rte. 63, 1 mi south of Rte. 12, Bryce* ☎435/834–5180 *or* 888/279–2304 ⊕*www.bryceviewlodge.com* ⇆*160 rooms* ⚿*In-hotel: some pets allowed* ▭*AE, D, DC, MC, V*

$ 🖼**Harold's Place.** Some of the modest cabins at this roadside resting spot still have that fresh wood smell as if they were just hammered together. The cabins are straightforward—two beds and a sink and toilet—but cozy in a spartan way. The complex is on Highway 12, a National Scenic Byway that bypasses the entrance to Bryce National Park. At this writing, rumor had it that the on-site restaurant may be closing. **Pros:** first place to stop on Highway 12 as you head east to Bryce, cabins are fun for families. **Cons:** erratic service, lack of services nearby, farther from the park than other properties. ⊠*3066 Hwy. Rte. 12, Panguitch* ☎435/ 676–2350 ⇆*20 cabins* ⚿*In-hotel: restaurant, pool, no elevator* ▭*AE, D, DC, MC, V.*

WHERE TO CAMP

Campgrounds in Bryce Canyon family-friendly and drive-in, except for the handful of backcountry sites that only backpackers and gung-ho day hikers ever see. Most campgrounds are first-come, first-served in high season. That said call and check about making reservations; slots fill up fast, particularly in summer, so book ahead when you can.

Most of the area's state parks have camping facilities, and Dixie National Forest contains many wonderful sites. Campgrounds may close seasonally because of lack of services (one loop of North Campground remains open year-round), and roads may occasionally close in winter while heavy snow is cleared.

WHAT IT COSTS				
¢	$$	$	$$$	$$$$
under $8	$15–$20	$8–$14	$21–$25	over $25

Camping prices are for campsites including a tent area, fire pit, bear-proof food-storage box, picnic table; potable water and pit toilets or restrooms will be nearby.

IN THE PARK

$$ ⚠**North Campground.** A cool, shady retreat in a forest of ponderosa pines, this is a great home base for your exploration of Bryce Canyon. You're near the general store, Bryce Canyon Lodge, trailheads, and the visitor center. Reservations are accepted for 32 sites from May through September; you can make them online up to 240 days in advance. Otherwise, spots are available on a first-come, first-served basis. The campground usually fills by early afternoon in July, August, and September. ✉*Main park road, ½ mi south of visitor center* ☎*435/834–5322* ⊕*www. recreation.gov 47 RV sites, 57 tent sites* ⚑*Flush toilets, dump station, drinking water, fire grates, picnic tables, public telephone, general store* ▭*No credit cards* ⊙*Open year-round.*

$$ ⚠**Sunset Campground.** This serene alpine campground is within walking distance of Bryce Canyon Lodge and many trailheads. All sites are available on a first-come, first-served basis. The campground fills by early afternoon in July, August, and September, so get your campsite before you sightsee. ✉*Main park road, 2 mi south of visitor center* ☎*435/834–5322* ⚑*101 sites, 49 for RVs* ⚑*Flush toilets, dump station, drinking water, fire grates, picnic tables, public telephone, general store* ▭*No credit cards* ⊙*May–Oct.*

OUTSIDE THE PARK

$$$– **Fodor'sChoice** ⚠**Best Western Ruby's Inn Campground and RV**
$$$ **Park.** North of the entrance to Bryce Canyon National Park, this campground sits amid pine and fir trees. RV sites, tepees, cabins, and tent sites are available. ✉ *Rte. 63, 1 mi off Hwy. 12, Bryce* ☎ *866/866–6616* ⊕ *www.brycecanyon campgrounds.com* ⚑*200 sites; 5 cabins, 8 tepees* ⚑*Flush toilets, full hookups, dump station, drinking water, guest laundry, showers, grills, picnic tables, electricity, public telephone, general store, swimming (pool)* ▭ *AE, D, DC, MC, V* ⊙ *Apr.–Oct.*

$$$– ⚠**Bryce Valley KOA.** This campground has the lowest (and
$$$$ warmest) elevation of any camping spot near Bryce Canyon.
☋ Everything you need for a quiet night of sleep and comfort is right here, near the slot canyons of the Paria River. There's a cooking pavilion for group get-togethers. ✉*Hwy. 12, at Red Rock Rd. (the Kodachrome Basin turn-off), Cannon-ville* ☎*435/679–8988 or 888/562–4710* ⊕*www.koa.com*

7

CAMPING IN AND AROUND BRYCE CANYON

Campground Name	Total # of Sites	# of RV sites	# of hook-ups	Drive-to sites	Hike-to sites	Flush toilets	Pit toilets	Drinking water	Showers	Fire grates/pits	Swimming	Boat access	Playground	Dump station	Ranger station	Public telephone	Reservations Possible	Daily fee per site	Dates open
Best Western Ruby's Inn Campground & RV Park	273	200	200	Y		Y		Y	Y	Y	Y			Y		Y	Y	$24–$39	Apr–Oct
Bryce Valley KOA	85	65	65	Y		Y		Y	Y	Y	Y		Y	Y		Y	Y	$20–$34	May–Sept
Bryce Canyon Pines Campground	40	26	26	Y		Y		Y	Y	Y	Y		Y			Y	Y	$17–$25	Apr–Nov
North Campground (in the park)	104	47		Y		Y		Y		Y			Y	Y		Y	Y	$15	Y/R
Sunset Campground (in the park)	101	49		Y		Y		Y		Y			Y	Y		Y	Y	$15	May–Oct
Red Canyon Campground	37	37		Y		Y		Y	Y	Y			Y	Y		Y	Y	$12	Y/R
Riverside Resort	100	65	65	Y		Y		Y	Y	Y	Y		Y	Y		Y	Y	$15–$28	Y/R

Y/R = year-round ** = Summer Only

🛏️65 RV sites, 20 tent sites, 5 cabins ♿Flush toilets, full hookups, dump station, drinking water, laundry facilities, showers, fire grates, grills, picnic tables, electricity, public telephone, general store, play area, swimming (pool) ▭AE, D, MC, V ⊙Mar.–Nov.

$$–$$$ 🏕️**Bryce Canyon Pines Campground.** This campground, 6 mi northwest of the park entrance is shady, quiet, and on the grounds of the Bryce Canyon Pines Resort. ✉ *Hwy. 12, Bryce* ☎435/834–5441 or 800/892–7923 ⊕ *www.bryce canyonmotel.com/campground* 🛏️40 sites, 26 with hookups ♿Flush toilets, full hookups, drinking water, showers, fire grates, electricity, public telephone, play area, swimming (pool) ▭D, DC, MC, V ⊙Apr.–Nov.

$ 🏕️**Red Canyon Campground / Dixie National Forest.** One of the nicest campgrounds in the Dixie National Forest, this ponderosa-shaded site is across from the Red Canyon Visitor's Center. The campground is open year-round, conditions permitting; reservations aren't accepted, though. ✉*Rte. 12, 10 mi northwest of Bryce Canyon National Park entrance* ☎435/676–9300 ⊕*www.fs.fed.us/r4/dixie* 🛏️37 sites, 1 group site ♿Flush toilets, drinking water, showers, fire grates, electricity, playground ▭No credit cards ⊙Open year-round.

$$–$$$ 🏕️**Riverside Resort.** As its name suggests, many of the sites here are on the banks of the Sevier River, making this a great spot to call home for a few days. You can play or fish in the river on hot summer days, and a large meadow accommodates overflow tent camping. A small motel is on-site. ✉*U.S. 89, 15 mi south of Panguitch, Hatch* ☎ 435/735–4223 or 800/824–5651 ⊕ *www.riversideresort-utah.com* 🛏️65 full hookups, unlimited tent camping ♿Flush toilets, dump station, drinking water, showers, grills, electricity, public telephone, general store, playground, swimming (river) ▭ D, MC, V ⊙Open year-round.

What's Nearby

WITH GRAND STAIRCASE–ESCALANTE
NATIONAL MONUMENT

WORD OF MOUTH

"Cedar City is about the same distance and travel time to Springdale as St. George. It is a bit closer to the Kolob Canyon section of Zion, and probably about 30 minutes or so closer to Bryce than St. George. The drive between Cedar City and Bryce would be much better (scenery-wise) in fall than from Zion to Bryce. Cedar Breaks National Monument is not far from Cedar City and should be nice in fall, provided there isn't an early snowfall."

—BibE1

Updated
by Steve
Pastorino

ZION AND BRYCE NATIONAL PARKS are the dual center-pieces of a massive southern Utah wilderness stretching from Arizona's Grand Canyon to I–70, which crosses the center of the state. The two parks are among the most recognized natural wonders in the Western United States, but they're also just a microcosm of the state's geological and topographical diversity. So get out there and explore.

The state's lowest point, Beaver Dam Wash, is here, south and west of St. George, while the Pine Valley Mountains north of that growing city are among the tallest in Utah. The region is often perceived as a hot, dry place, yet from the desert depths you can see snowy peaks and evergreens.

Utah Scenic Byway 12 delivers you to Bryce Canyon's front door, but also connects you to Grand Staircase–Escalante National Monument, the second-largest National Monument in the lower 48 at 1.7 million acres. Set aside by President Bill Clinton in 1996, the monument is fraught with the typical Western controversy that pits private landowners, miners, and developers against the Bureau of Land Management—but undeniably is a treasure trove of geological and archaeological sites (as many as 100,000 unique treasures).

This is a land of adventure and contemplation, of adrenaline and retreat. It's not an either-or proposition; you rejuvenate whether soaking at a luxury spa or careening on a mountain bike down an alpine single-track. The land once tamed for planting cotton and fruit is now a playground for golfers, bikers, and hikers. Arts festivals and concerts under canyon walls have smoothed the rough edges hewn by miners and the boomtowns that evaporated as quickly as they materialized. Ruins, petroglyphs, pioneer graffiti, and ghost towns—monuments to what once was—beckon new explorers. The region's secrets reveal themselves to seekers, yet some mysteries remain elusive—the paradox of the bustling world that lies hidden under the impression of spare, silent, and open space.

Such contrasts have always attracted the curious. Famed explorer John Wesley Powell charted the uncharted; the young idealist and dreamer Everett Reuss left his well-to-do family and lost himself without a trace in the canyons; the author and curmudgeon Ed Abbey found himself, and has since been thought of, depending on whom you ask, as either a voice crying in the wilderness or a pariah in Pareah. But that's the beauty of this place, the joy of choice in a land that confronts and challenges. We come, ostensibly, to escape; yet we really come to discover.

CEDAR BREAKS NATIONAL MONUMENT. About 22 mi east of Cedar City, and 60 mi west of Bryce Canyon, Cedar Breaks is a plateau at 10,000 feet above sea level with a giant amphitheater of red rocks like Bryce. Its visitor center was constructed in 1937 and is listed on the National Register of Historic Places. The monument is known for its hiking, camping, and wildflowers.

GATEWAYS TO ZION NATIONAL PARK

Hotels, restaurants, and shops keep popping up in **Springdale,** which has undoubtedly surpassed its 2000 census count of 457 residents. On the southern boundary of Zion National Park, the town still manages to maintain its small-town charm—and oh, the view! There are a surprising number of wonderful places to stay and eat, and if you take the time to stroll the main drag, or make use of frequent shuttle stops, you can find some great shops and galleries. For listings in Springdale, *see "Zion Hikes & Activities" and "Where to Stay & Eat in Zion."*

On Route 9 between St. George and Zion stands the small town of **Hurricane,** population 8,250. Pronounced "HUR-aken," this community on the Virgin River has experienced enormous growth, probably owing to the boom in nearby St. George. Hurricane is home to one of Utah's most scenic 18-hole golf courses and is a less expensive and less crowded base for exploring Zion National Park.

Farther afield, the booming city of **St. George** offers a regional airport and every imaginable service from resort hotels to a variety of restaurants, a state university, and myriad cultural activities. At 40 mi to the Zion National Park entrance, it's a viable base for exploration of the region. The Mormon settlement turned retirement community turned sunbelt hub is also minutes away from legalized gambling in Mesquite, Nevada. Don't miss Snow Canyon State Park just north of the city.

On Route 9, 13 mi to the east of the park, is **Mt. Carmel Junction,** an intersection offering some funky small-town lodging and the don't-miss studio of Maynard Dixon, the artist many consider the finest painter of the American West. Other nearby towns, much smaller in size, include Virgin, La Verkin, and the ghost town of **Grafton,** where

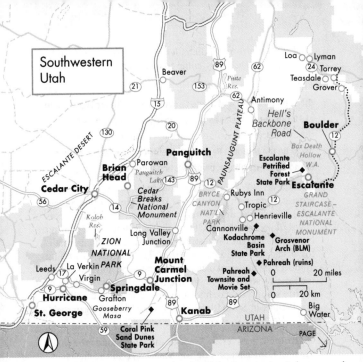

there's only a stone school and dusty cemetery. It has starred in films such as *Butch Cassidy and the Sundance Kid*.

GATEWAYS TO BRYCE CANYON
NATIONAL PARK

Decent amenities, inexpensive lodging (mainly strip motels), and an excellent location 24 mi northwest of Bryce Canyon National Park on U.S. 89 make **Panguitch** a launching pad for recreation in the area. The town is noted for the distinctive brick architecture of its early homes and outbuildings, and for the original facades of some of its late-19th-century Main Street commercial structures.

About 47 mi northeast of Bryce, **Escalante** has modern amenities and a state park like nothing else in Utah. It's also a western gateway to the Grand Staircase–Escalante National Monument. If you're traveling through southwestern Utah on Interstate 15, **Cedar City** will be your exit to Bryce. The largest city you'll encounter in this part of Utah, it's 78 mi from Bryce Canyon. The city's claims to fame are its popular Utah Shakespearean Festival and a major state university, and it's also steeped in Mormon pioneer heritage.

CEDAR CITY

*18 mi from Kolob Canyons section of Zion National Park
and 58 mi from Springdale (south entrance to park), about
70 mi west of Bryce Canyon.*

Rich iron-ore deposits here grabbed Mormon leader
Brigham Young's attention, and he ordered a Church of
Jesus Christ of Latter-day Saints (LDS) mission established.
The first ironworks and foundry opened in 1851 and operated for only eight years; problems with the furnace, flooding, and hostility between settlers and Native Americans
eventually put out the flame. Residents then turned to
ranching and agriculture for their livelihood, and Cedar
City thrived thereafter. Cedar City calls itself "The Festival
City." The Southern Utah University campus hosts the city's
major event, the Tony Award–winning Utah Shakespearean
Festival, which has been stretching its season longer and
longer as its reputation has grown. Though better known
for festivals than recreation, the city is well placed for
exploring the Brian Head summer and ski resort area.

WHAT TO SEE

Inside the Iron County Visitor Center, the **Daughters of the
Utah Pioneers Museum** displays pioneer artifacts such as an
old trundle sewing machine, an antique four-poster bed, and
photographs of old Cedar City and its inhabitants. ⊠*582
N. Main St.* ☎*435/586–4484* ⊠*Free* ⊙*Weekdays 1–4.*

The **Iron Mission State Park Museum** is a memorial to the
county's iron-industry heritage. Explore the bullet-scarred
stagecoach that ran in the days of Butch Cassidy, plus tools
and other mining artifacts. A log cabin built in 1851—the
oldest standing home in southern Utah—and a collection of wagon wheels and farm equipment is displayed
outside. Local artisans demonstrate pioneer crafts. ⊠*635
N. Main St.* ☎*435/586–9290* ⊕*www.stateparks.utah.gov*
⊠*$3* ⊙*Mid-May–mid-Sept., daily 9–6; mid-Sept.–Oct. and
Mar.–mid-May, daily 9–5; Nov.–Feb., Mon.–Sat. 9–5.*

The large, beehive-shaped charcoal kiln is the most complete and distinctive remnant of **Old Iron Town,** founded
in the late 1860s and the site of southern Utah's second
attempt to produce iron. A quick, self-guided walking
tour passes the remains of a furnace, a foundry, and a
mule-powered grinding stone called a "Spanish erastra,"
used to process ore. The town closed when the iron operations ceased in 1877. ⊠*On Rte. 56, 25 mi west of Cedar
City* ☎*435/586–9290* ⊠*Free.*

8

SPORTS & THE OUTDOORS

Every June, more than 7,000 Utahans compete in everything from archery to horseshoes, arm wrestling, basketball, and gymnastics during the **Utah Summer Games** (☎*435/865–8421 or 800/354–4849*) at Southern Utah University.

The **Dixie National Forest** (✉*1789 N. Wedgewood La.* ☎*435/865–3700* ⊕*www.fs.fed.us/dxnf*) administers an area encompassing almost 2 million acres, stretching 170 mi across southwestern Utah, and containing 26 designated campgrounds. The forest is popular for such activities as horseback riding, fishing, and hiking.

HIKING

Join **Southern Utah Scenic Tours** (☎*435/867–8690 or 888/ 404–8687* ⊕*www.utahscenictours.com*) for an all-day tour from Cedar City to either Zion National Park or Bryce National Park, including a short, easy-to-moderate hike. The price includes pick-up and drop-off at your hotel; snacks and lunch; and all applicable park fees.

WHERE TO EAT

¢ ✕**Bulloch Drug.** *American.* Swivel onto a stool in front of the circa-1942 soda fountain and cool off as the old timers did, with soda syrup hand-mixed with carbonated water right before you. Maybe your grandparents would remember Ironport, a soft drink from the '30s described here as a "spicy cream soda." There are shakes, malts, floats, and banana splits, too. ✉*91 N. Main St.* ☎*435/586–9651* ▭*AE, D, MC, V* ⊙*Closed Sun.*

$ ✕**Market Grill.** *American.* A low-slung, ranch-style building next to the Cedar City stockyard, this place has vinyl-bench booths and a rutted dirt parking area well suited to the pickup trucks that usually park here, attesting to its popularity amongst locals. The fare is just as basic: burgers, barbecued ribs, and a salad bar. ✉*2290 W. 200 North St.* ☎*435/586–9325* ▭*MC, V* ⊙*Closed Sun.*

$$–$$$ ✕**Milt's Stage Stop.** *American.* This dinner spot in beautiful
★ Cedar Canyon is known for its 12-ounce rib-eye steak, prime rib, fresh crab, lobster, and shrimp dishes. In winter, deer feed in front of the restaurant as a fireplace blazes away inside. A number of hunting trophies decorate the rustic building's interior, and splendid views of the surrounding mountains delight patrons year-round. ✉*Cedar Canyon, 5 mi east of town on Rte. 14* ☎*435/586–9344* ▭*AE, D, DC, MC, V* ⊙*No lunch.*

¢ ✕**The Pastry Pub.** *Café.* Don't be fooled by the name—coffee and tea are the only brews on tap here, and sandwiches and salads join pastries on the chalkboard menu. Build a sandwich of meat, egg, cheese, and more on a bagel, croissant, sliced bread, or one of five flavors of wraps. Festival goers, take note: this is the best bet for a late-night bite after the show. ⊠*86 W. Center St.* ☎*435/867–1400* ☐*AE, D, MC, V* ⊘*Closed Sun.*

$$ ✕**Rusty's Ranch House.** *American.* Under the cliffs of Cedar Canyon, this Old West–style steak house dishes out meat and potatoes to hungry tourists and locals. The specialties include petit filet mignon with coconut shrimp, creamy chicken pasta, and homemade bread pudding. ⊠*Cedar Canyon, 2 mi east of town on Rte. 14* ☎*435/586–3839* ☐*AE, D, DC, MC, V* ⊘*Closed Sun. No lunch.*

WHERE TO STAY

$ ▨**Abbey Inn.** This two-story property has somewhat dim but spacious rooms with balconies. Some suites have kitchens, and the elegant honeymoon suite has an in-room spa. Walk to nearby restaurants and the Utah Shakespearean Festival, all of which are a few blocks away. An airport shuttle is available. **Pros:** easy access to I–15 and Shakespeare festival, hot breakfast, ski packages in winter. **Cons:** some guests think rooms are too dark. ⊠*940 W. 200 North St.* ☎*435/586–9966 or 800/325–5411* ⊕*www.abbeyinncedar.com* ➷*80 rooms* ⌂*In-room: refrigerator, Internet. In-hotel: pool, laundry facilities, no-smoking rooms* ☐*AE, D, DC, MC, V* ⦿*CP.*

$ ▨**Bard's Inn Bed & Breakfast.** Rooms in this restored turn-of-the-20th-century house are named after heroines and heroes in Shakespeare's plays. There are antiques throughout and handcrafted quilts grace the beds. Hosts Jack and Audrey prepare a full breakfast that includes fresh home-baked breads such as Amish friendship bread and croissants, plus fruit, juices, and shirred eggs. Bone up on your Shakespeare before attending a play by reading from a supply of on-site Cliff Notes. **Pros:** close to the festival grounds, dining options nearby, airport shuttle available. **Cons:** rooms fill up in advance during festival season. ⊠*150 S. 100 West St.* ☎*435/586–6612* ⊕*www.bardsbandb.com* ➷*7 rooms* ⌂*In-room: no phone, refrigerator (some), Wi-Fi. In-hotel: Internet terminal, Wi-Fi, no-smoking rooms* ☐*AE, MC, V.*

8

$-$$ 🖥**Best Western Town & Country Inn.** Actually two buildings directly across the street from each other, this two-story motel has good amenities and a friendly staff. You can easily walk the few blocks to the Shakespearean Festival and the downtown shopping district. **Pros:** conveniently located near downtown, airport shuttle available. **Cons:** can get crowded during festival season. ⊠*189 N. Main St.* ☎*435/586–9900 or 800/493–4089* ⊕*www.bwtowncoun try.com* ⟋*157 rooms* ⚴*In-room: refrigerator, Internet (some), Wi-Fi. In-hotel: 2 restaurants, pools, laundry facilities, no-smoking rooms* ⊟*AE, D, DC, MC, V* ⃝❘CP.

¢–$ 🖥**Willow Glen Inn.** Staying on this 8.5-acre farm is like staying at grandma's. Three buildings (including the converted pony barn) contain rooms, no two alike, which have details like flowered quilts and aspen wood trim. **Pros:** family-owned B&B with unique rooms. **Cons:** no services in immediate vicinity. ⊠*3308 N. Bulldog Rd., Enoch, UT* ☎*435/ 586–3275* ⊕*www.willowgleninn.com* ⟋*10 rooms* ⚴*In-room: no phone. In-hotel: no-smoking rooms* ⊟*AE, D, DC, MC, V* ⃝❘BP.

THE ARTS

★ Fodor'sChoice From June to October, the **Utah Shakespearean Festival** (☎*435/586–7880 or 800/752–9849* ⊕*www.bard.org*) puts on plays by the Bard and others, drawing tens of thousands over the course of the season. The outdoor theater at Southern Utah University is a replica of the Old Globe Theatre and showcases Shakespearean costumes and sets during the season. Call ahead for a schedule of performances.

Held at Municipal Park in Cedar City during the July peak of the Utah Shakespearean Festival, the **Mid-Summer Renaissance Faire** (☎*435/586–6757 or 435/586–1124* ⊕*www. umrf.net*) provides entertainment such as fencing demonstrations, belly dancing, games, and crafts, and offers lots of food.

The **Canyon Country Western Arts Festival** (☎*800/354–4849*) brings the heritage of the Old West to life on the campus of Southern Utah University every March. Leather-working, blacksmithing, and other Western crafts demonstrations mix with traditional cowboy poetry and music.

Traditional Paiute music and a parade are part of the **Paiute Restoration Gathering and Powwow** (☎*435/586–1112*), held in June at different locations on Paiute tribal lands.

SHOPPING

Shop off the beaten path at **The Wizz** (✉ *490 S. Main St.* ☎ *435/586–7113*), in Cedar City's downtown historic district, for incense, oils, and jewelry. The store also rents costumes.

ST. GEORGE

40 mi southwest of Zion National Park via I–15 and Rte. 9.

Believing the mild year-round climate ideal for growing cotton, Brigham Young dispatched 309 LDS families in 1861 to found St. George. They were to raise cotton and silkworms and to establish a textile industry, to make up for textile shortages resulting from the Civil War. The area was subsequently dubbed "Utah's Dixie," a name that stuck even after the war ended and the "other" South could once again provide cotton to Utah. The settlers—many of them originally from southern states—found the desert climate preferable to northern Utah's snow, and they remained as farmers and ranchers. Crops included fruit, molasses, and grapes for wine that the pioneers sold to nearby mining communities. St. Georgians now number more than 60,000, many of whom are retirees attracted by the hot, dry climate and the numerous golf courses. But historic Ancestor Square, the city's many well-preserved, original pioneer and Mormon structures, and a growing shopping district make St. George a popular destination for families, as well.

Numbers in the margin correspond to the St. George map.

Many of the Mormons who settled in southwestern Utah in 1861 were converts from Switzerland, and the nearby small town of Santa Clara, northwest of St. George, celebrates this heritage every September during the **Santa Clara Swiss Days** (☎ *435/673–6712*), which includes crafts and food booths, games, a parade, and a tour of historic homes.

WHAT TO SEE

❶ **Brigham Young Winter Home.** Mormon leader Brigham Young spent the last five winters of his life in the warm, sunny climate of St. George. Built of adobe on a sandstone-and-basalt foundation, Young's home has been restored to its original condition. His portrait hangs over one fireplace, and furnishings authentic to the late-19th-century time

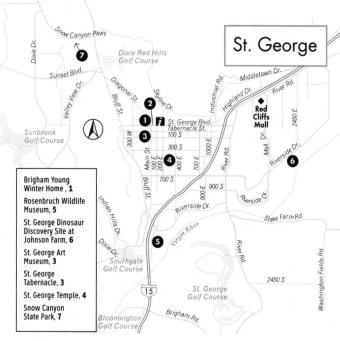

period have been donated by supporters. Guided tours are
available. ⊠*67 W. 200 North St.* ☎*435/673–5181* ⬛*Free*
⊙*Daily 9–6.*

❺ Rosenbruch Wildlife Museum. Chances are this museum is
★ unlike any you've ever seen. This modern 25,000-square-
foot facility displays more than 300 species of wildlife
(stuffed) from around the globe, displayed in an uncanny
representation of their native habitat—the plains of Africa,
the forests of North America, and the mountains of Asia.
A wheelchair-accessible pathway of almost ¼ mi winds
through the different environments. Two waterfalls cascade
from a two-story mountain, and more than 50 hidden speak-
ers provide ambient wildlife and nature sounds. Before your
tour, check out the video presentation in the 200-seat theater,
and be sure not to miss the massive bug collection. ⊠*1835
Convention Center Dr.* ☎*435/656–0033* ⊕*www.rosenbruch.
org* ⬛*$8* ⊙*Mon. noon–9, Tues.–Sat. 10–6.*

❼ Snow Canyon State Park. Red Navajo sandstone mesas and
★ formations are crowned with black lava rock, creating
high-contrast vistas from either end of the park. From the
campground you can scramble up huge sandstone mounds

and overlook the entire valley. ⊠*1002 Snow Canyon Dr., Ivins, 8 mi northwest of St. George* ☎*435/628–2255* ⊕*www.stateparks.utah.gov* ⊠*$5* ⊙*Daily 6 AM–10 PM.*

② **St. George Art Museum.** Spend a few quiet hours out of the Dixie sun at the city's art museum. The permanent collection celebrates local potters, photographers, painters, and more. Special exhibits highlight local history. ⊠*47 E. 200 North St.* ☎*435/627–4525* ⊕*www.sgcity.org/artmuseum/* ⊠*$3* ⊙*Mon. 1–8 PM, Tues.–Sat. 10–5.*

⑥ **St. George Dinosaur Discovery Site at Johnson Farm.** You can
ℭ follow footsteps cast in stone millions of years ago at the Johnson Farm, where property development came to a halt when the ancient prints from the Jurassic period were unearthed in 2000. An active archaeological dig, this site is entrancing to children. To reach the tracks, take 700 South Street east to Foremaster Drive and continue past the sod farm. ⊠*2180 E. Riverside Dr.* ☎*435/574–3466* ⊕*www.dinotrax.com* ⊠*$3* ⊙*Mon.–Sat. 10–6.*

③ **St. George Tabernacle.** Mormon settlers began work on the tabernacle in June 1863, a few months after the city of St. George was established. Upon completion of the sandstone building's 140-foot clock tower 13 years later, Brigham Young formally dedicated the site. This is one of the best-preserved pioneer buildings in the entire state, and is still used for public meetings and programs for the entire community. ⊠*18 S. Main St.* ☎*435/673–5181* ⊙*Daily 9–6.*

④ **St. George Temple.** The red-sandstone temple, plastered over with white stucco, was completed in 1877 and served as a meeting place for both Mormons and other congregations. It's still in use today, and though only Mormons can enter the temple, a visitor center next door offers guided tours for everyone. ⊠*250 E. 400 South St.* ☎*435/673–5181* ⊠*Free* ⊙*Visitor center daily 9–9.*

SPORTS & THE OUTDOORS

BIKING

The folks at **Bicycles Unlimited** (⊠*90 S. 100 East St.* ☎*888/673–4492* ⊕*www.bicyclesunlimited.com*) are a font of information on mountain biking in southern Utah. They rent bikes and sell parts, accessories, and guidebooks.

GOLF

Bloomington (⊠*3174 E. Bloomington Dr.* ☎*435/673–2029*) offers a striking combination of manicured fairways and greens beneath sandstone cliffs.

Dixie Red Hills (⊠*645 W. 1250 North St.* ☎*435/634–5852*) has 9 holes.

The 18-hole **Entrada** (⊠*2537 W. Entrada Trail* ☎*435/986–2200*) is Utah's first Johnny Miller Signature Course.

St. George Golf Club (⊠*2190 S. 1400 East St.* ☎*435/634–5854*) is a popular 18-hole course with challenging par-3 holes.

Water provides challenges at **Southgate Golf Club** (⊠*1975 S. Tonaquint Dr.* ☎*435/628–0000*), with several holes bordering ponds or crossing the Santa Clara River.

Designed by Ted Robinson, fairway features at **Sunbrook** (⊠*2366 Sunbrook Dr.* ☎*435/634–5866*) include rock walls, lakes, and waterfalls.

HIKING

Snow Canyon State Park (⊠*8 mi northwest of St. George on Rte. 18* ☎*435/628–2255* ⊕*www.stateparks.utah.gov*) has several short trails and lots of small desert canyons to explore.

WHERE TO EAT

$ ✕**Bear Paw Coffee Company.** *American.* The menu is full of
★ flavor, with elements of Southwestern, Tex-Mex, American, and Italian cuisines all represented, but breakfast is the star of the show here (served all day, every day). The coffee is hot, the teas loose, the juice fresh, and the servers smiling. Home brewers (of coffee and tea, that is) can get their fresh beans and leaves here, too. ⊠*75 N. Main St.* ☎*435/634–0126* ⊟*AE, D, MC, V* ⊗*No dinner.*

¢ ✕**Irmita's Mexican Food.** *Mexican.* Locals recommend this fruit-stand-turned-diner for its inexpensive Mexican fare. The selection is simple and no-nonsense—three items, three fillings, beans, and rice—but three temperatures of salsa (try the spicy "ooh la la") plus cabbage and lime round out a fine meal that proves cheap can be satisfying. The tiny dining room fills quickly, and the open kitchen's grill brings the St. George heat inside, but you can also sit outside at tables beneath palm-frond umbrellas. ⊠*515 S. Bluff St.* ☎*435/652–0161* ⊟*No credit cards* ⊗*Closed Sun. No dinner Mon.*

$$$ ✕**Painted Pony.** *Contemporary.* Patio dining and local art hanging on the walls provide suave accompaniment to the creative meals served in this downtown restaurant. Be sure to try the Dixie pork chop or the bacon-wrapped duck. ⊠*2 W. St. George Blvd., Ancestor Sq.* ☎*435/634–1700* ⊕*www.painted-pony.com* ⊟*AE, D, MC, V* ⊘*No lunch Sun.*

$ ✕**Panama Grill.** *Southwestern.* This restaurant serves New Mexican–style cuisine and one of the best fish tacos in town. There's open-air dining on the patio, and you can temper the St. George summer heat with an excellent margarita. ⊠*2 W. St. George Blvd., Ancestor Sq.* ☎*435/673-7671* ⊟*AE, D, DC, MC, V* ⊘*Closed Sun.*

$–$$ ✕**Pancho & Lefty's.** *Mexican.* Locals come to this lively restaurant hung with sombreros and colorful blankets for the flautas (rolled, fried tortillas stuffed with meats and vegetables), chimichangas, sizzling fajitas, and ice-cold margaritas. ⊠*1050 S. Bluff St.* ☎*435/628–4772* ⊟*AE, D, MC, V.*

$$$– ✕**Sullivan's Rococo Steakhouse & Inn.** *American.* Specializing
$$$$ in beef and seafood, this St. George restaurant is known for its prime rib, but its vistas are worth noting, too. It sits atop a hill overlooking town, so you can enjoy spectacular views right from your table. ⊠*511 Airport Rd.* ☎*435/628–3671* ⊕*www.rococo.net/steakhouse.html* ⊟*AE, D, MC, V.*

WHERE TO STAY

$$ ⊤**Best Western Coral Hills.** The town's walking tour of historic pioneer buildings begins a block from this motel, which is next to the old courthouse and close to many restaurants. You can spend a hot afternoon relaxing in the shade of palm trees next to the outdoor pool. **Pros:** walking distance to downtown attractions, airport shuttle is available. **Cons:** high-traffic location. ⊠*125 E. St. George Blvd.* ☎*435/673–4844 or 800/542–7733* ⊕*www.coralhills.com* ⊋*95 rooms, 3 suites* ⚬*In-room: refrigerator, DVD (some), Internet (some), Wi-Fi. In-hotel: pools, gym, laundry facilities, laundry service, Wi-Fi, no-smoking rooms* ⊟*AE, D, DC, MC, V* ⊙*CP.*

$–$$ ⊤**Comfort Suites.** Two blocks from the Dixie Convention Center, this hotel's "minisuites" have comfortable sitting areas and large TVs. The shaded outdoor common areas offer additional space in good weather. **Pros:** great location for conventioneers, airport shuttle is available. **Cons:** too far from downtown to walk. ✉*1239 S. Main St.* ☎*435/ 673–7000* ⊕*www.stgeorgecomfortsuites.com* ➾*122 suites* ⌂*In-room: refrigerator, Wi-Fi. In-hotel: pool, gym, laundry facilities, laundry service, Internet terminal, no-smoking rooms* ⊟*AE, D, DC, MC, V* ⍾*CP.*

$–$$$$ 🖭**Green Gate Village Historic Inn.** Step back in time in these
★ restored pioneer homes dating to the 1860s. The inn takes its name from the green gates and fences that surrounded the homes of St. George's LDS leaders in the late 1800s. The last remaining original gate is displayed in the inn's garden and served as a model for those now surrounding Green Gate Village. Behind the gates is a village of nine fully restored pioneer homes filled with antique furnishings and modern amenities. Guests with children need to get prior approval from the management. **Pros:** each building is the real historic deal, location is close to tabernacle and downtown walking tour. **Cons:** villagelike setting might not appeal to those seeking privacy. ✉*76 W. Tabernacle St.* ☎*435/628–6999 or 800/350–6999* ⊕*www.greengate villageinn.com* ➾*4 rooms, 10 suites* ⌂*In-room: kitchen (some), refrigerator, DVD (some), Wi-Fi (some). In-hotel: 2 restaurants, room service, pool, gym, spa, Internet terminal, parking (no fee), no-smoking rooms* ⊟*AE, D, MC, V* ⍾*BP.*

$$$$ 🖭**Green Valley Spa & Tennis Resort.** Minutes from downtown but in a world of its own, this serene, luxurious resort and inn consistently ranks among the best in the world. Here you can arrange your days around morning hikes, golf or tennis lessons, exercise classes, massage therapy, facials, and delicious low-calorie meals. All meals, and some spa services, are included in the weekly rate. Dozens of fitness classes are offered, as well as guided treks into the red rock canyon country surrounding the resort. A three-day minimum stay is required. **Pros:** fourteen tennis courts, seven swimming pools, and a 4,000-square-foot gym pamper athletes. **Cons:** setting is adult-oriented (which may not be a negative for some), children under 10 not allowed in dining room. ✉*1871 W. Canyon View Dr.* ☎*435/628–8060 or 800/237–1068* ⊕*www.greenvalleyspa.com* ➾*45 suites* ⌂*In-room: safe, refrigerator, Internet, Wi-Fi. In-hotel: restaurant, golf course, tennis courts, pools, gym, spa, laundry service, parking (no fee), some pets allowed, no-smoking rooms* ⊟*AE, D, MC, V* ⍾*FAP.*

$ 🖥**Ramada Inn.** On St. George's major thoroughfare and within a mile of restaurants, shopping, and the historic district, this is one of the city's most convenient properties. The rooms and furnishings are up-to-date and comfortable. **Pros:** convenient (by car) to highway, town, restaurants, and shopping, kids love the pool. **Cons:** don't go for a walk due to the busy off-ramp/intersection. ⊠*1440 E. St. George Blvd.* ☎*435/628–2828 or 888/704–8476* ⊕*www.ramada inn.net* ⤴*136 rooms* ♿*Refrigerator (some), microwave (some), Wi-Fi. In-hotel: pool, laundry service, no-smoking rooms* ☐*AE, D, DC, MC, V* ⊙*CP.*

★ Fodor'sChoice 🖥**Red Mountain Spa.** Near the mouth of Snow
$$$$ Canyon, this active resort is a retreat designed for fitness and rejuvenation. Breakfast and lunch buffets list the nutritional contents of each item, while dinner is a more traditional sit-down experience. But it's not just about the food; there are fitness classes, hikes, yoga, and plenty of other activities that leave you with a healthy glow. The well-appointed rooms aren't especially large, but with so many things to do, you won't want to lounge around your room anyway. **Pros:** down-to-earth spa experience, healthy food, airport shuttle available. **Cons:** You might feel guilty if you don't wake up at dawn to hit the gym or the trails. ⊠*1275 E. Red Mountain Cir., Ivins, 7 mi northwest of St. George* ☎*435/673–4905 or 800/407–3002* ⊕*www.redmountain spa.com* ⤴*82 rooms, 24 suites* ♿*In-room: safe, Internet. In-hotel: 2 restaurants, tennis court, pools, gym, spa, water sports, bicycles, laundry facilities, Internet terminal, some pets allowed, no kids under 12, no-smoking rooms* ☐*AE, D, MC, V* ⊙*FAP.*

$–$$ 🖥**Seven Wives Inn Bed & Breakfast.** It's said that Brigham Young slept here, and that one of the buildings may have been a hiding place for polygamists after the practice was outlawed in the 1880s. In fact, the inn is named for an ancestor of the owner who indeed had seven wives. Not surprisingly the rooms are named after those wives. Antiques are liberally placed throughout the rooms, which are elaborately decorated with flowers and pastels. One room has a jetted tub installed in a Model T Ford. In-room spa treatments are available (an unexpected treat!). **Pros:** more than a century of history permeates the well-appointed rooms, walk to shops, restaurants, and sights of historic downtown. **Cons:** although kids are welcome, parents will fret as they dodge the antiques. ⊠*217 N. 100 West St.* ☎*800/600–3737* ⊕*www.sevenwivesinn.com* ⤴*9 rooms,*

4 suites &*In-room: refrigerator (some), DVD (some), Wi-Fi. In-hotel: pool, Wi-Fi, some pets allowed, no-smoking rooms* ⊟*AE, D, MC, V* †⊙†*BP.*

NIGHTLIFE & THE ARTS

NIGHTLIFE

Ask locals where to go for nightlife in this conservative city and they'll say, with a straight face, Mesquite, Nevada (almost 40 mi away). Then they'll remember the aptly named **The One & Only Watering Hole** (✉*800 E. St. George Blvd.* ☎*435/673–9191*), a beer-only joint in a strip mall with billiards, televised sports, and live music on many weekends.

THE ARTS

Artisan booths, food, children's activities, and entertainment, including cowboy poets, are all part of the **St. George Arts Festival** (☎*435/634–5942*), held the Friday and Saturday of Easter weekend.

Honoring southern Utah's cotton-growing heritage, St. George hosts beauty pageants, Dutch oven cook-offs, and a firefighter competition during May's **Washington Cotton Festival** (☎*435/634–9850*).

A rotating series of musicals such as *Joseph and the Amazing Technicolor Dream Coat* and *Les Misérables* entertain at **Tuacahn** (✉*1100 Tuacahn Dr., Ivins* ☎*435/652–3200 or 800/746–9882* ⊕ *www.tuacahn.org*), an outdoor amphitheater nestled in a natural sandstone cove.

SHOPPING

★ Historic **Ancestor Square** (✉*St. George Blvd. and Main St.* ☎*435/628–1658*) is the shopping and dining centerpiece of downtown St. George. Occupants of the tiny old Jailhouse Coffee now serve java instead of time, providing a pick-me-up from browsing the many galleries, shops, and restaurants.

Pick up recreational items that made the packing list but not the pack at the **Outdoor Outlet** (✉*1062 E. Tabernacle St.* ☎*435/628–3611 or 800/726–8106* ⊕ *www.outdooroutlet. com*). Shop for bargains at their frequent clearance sales.

The **Red Cliffs Mall** (✉*1770 E. Red Cliffs Dr.* ☎*435/673–0099* ⊕*www.redcliffsmall.com*) is a retail mall with more than 40 stores.

Zion Factory Stores (⊠*250 N. Red Cliffs Dr., I–15 Exit 8* ☎*435/674–9800* ⊕*www.zionfactorystores.com*) is southern Utah's only factory-outlet center.

HURRICANE

23 mi southwest of Zion Rte. 9 east and Rte. 17 south.

An increasing number of lodging establishments makes Hurricane a fine alternate base for exploring Dixie. Nearby Gooseberry Mesa rivals Moab as one of the best places to mountain bike in Utah.

SPORTS & THE OUTDOORS

BIKING

The mountain biking trails on **Gooseberry Mesa,** off Route 59 south of Hurricane, rival those of world-famous Moab on the other side of southern Utah, yet don't have the hordes of fat-tire fanatics. Come here for solitary and technical single-track challenges.

FESTIVALS

Classic cars from all over the West descend on Hurricane every March for the **Hurricane Easter Car Show** (☎*435/635–3402*), which attracts about 7,000 people each year.

GOLF

Hurricane has **Sky Mountain** (⊠*1030 N. 2600 West St.* ☎*888/345–5551*), one of the state's most scenic 18-hole golf courses. Many fairways are framed by red rock outcroppings; the course has a front-tee view of the nearby 10,000-foot Pine Valley Mountains.

WHERE TO EAT & STAY

¢ ✕**Main Street Café.** *American.* One of the best cups of coffee
★ in Dixie is poured right here in Hurricane. A full espresso bar will satisfy "caffiends," while vegetarians and others can choose from salads, sandwiches, breakfast burritos, homemade breads, and desserts. Sit inside to admire the works of local artists, or share the patio with the hummingbirds. ⊠*138 S. Main St.* ☎*435/635–9080* ⊟*MC, V* ⊘*Closed Sun. No dinner.*

¢ 🏨**Comfort Inn Zion.** Golfers will appreciate the package deals available with nearby courses, and everyone benefits from being fairly close to Zion National Park, which is a 35-mi drive away. If the hot southern Utah sun has sapped your energy, a dip in the pool will wake you for your next adventure. **Pros:** minutes from two 18-hole golf courses. **Cons:** location in a newly developed area lacks charm. ⊠*43 N. 2600 West* ☎*435/635–3500 or 800/635–3577* ⊕*www. comfortinnzion.com* ⊲*53 rooms* ⅍*In-room: Wi-Fi. In-hotel: pool, laundry facilities, Internet terminal, Wi-Fi, no-smoking rooms* ⊟*AE, D, MC, V* ⍩*CP.*

$ 🖵**Travelodge.** This basic motel will provide you with a comfortable night's rest if you want few other amenities, though there is a pool. It's a comfortable distance—a 35-mi drive—from Zion National Park. **Pros:** in the heart of downtown. **Cons:** there's not much to do in downtown Hurricane. ⊠*280 W. State St.* ☎*435/635–4647 or 800/578–7878* ⊕*www.travelodgezion.com* ⊲*62 rooms* ⅍*In-room: microwave, refrigerator, Wi-Fi. In-hotel: pool, spa, laundry facilities, Internet terminal, Wi-Fi, no-smoking rooms* ⊟*AE, D, MC, V* ⍩*CP.*

HATCH

21 mi from Bryce; 13 mi west on Hwy. 12 or 8 mi south on Hwy. 89.

Hatch gives anglers the best access to Tropic Reservoir, regarded as a favorite fishing hole in this part of the state. It's a quieter, more pleasant alternative to the one-stoplight town of Panguitch.

WHERE TO EAT

$ ✕**Café Adobe.** *Mexican.* Ask the locals for a unique meal in the Bryce area, and only one place is mentioned—Café Adobe. It's about 20 mi away in the tiny town of Hatch, but it's worth the drive. The Mexican menu delivers more flavors per bite than any "comfort food" restaurant in this part of Utah. The menu has a range of Mexican favorites, including enchiladas, fajitas, chimichangas, and tacos. The tasty rice and beans accompanies everything. Burgers and sandwiches receive high marks as well. ⊠*16 N. Main St., Hatch* ☎*435/743–4020 MC, V* ⊙*Closed Nov.–Mar.*

WHERE TO CAMP

$$–$$$ ⌂**Riverside Resort.** As its name suggests, many of the sites here are on the banks of the Sevier River, making this a great spot to call home for a few days. You can play or fish in the river on hot summer days, and a large meadow accommodates overflow tent camping. A small motel is also available on site for those who might not want to "rough it." ⊠*15*

*mi south of Panguitch on U.S. 89, Hatch ☎435/735–4223
or 800/824–5651 ⊕www.riversideresort-utah.com ⇄65
full hookups, unlimited tent camping ⏚Flush toilets, dump
station, drinking water, showers, electricity, public telephone,
general store, play area, swimming (river) ⊟D, MC, V.*

MT. CARMEL JUNCTION

*13 mi east of Zion National Park (east entrance) via Rte.
9 east.*

Little more than where Route 9 meets U.S. 89, Mt. Carmel Junction does offer some funky small-town lodging
for those willing to stay about 15 minutes east of Zion
National Park's east entrance. But don't miss the studio of
Maynard Dixon, the artist many consider the finest painter
of the American West.

The **Maynard Dixon Home and Studio** was the final residence
of the best-known painter of the American West, who died
here in 1946. The property and log cabin structure are now
maintained by the nonprofit Thunderbird Foundation for
the Arts, which gives tours and schedules artist workshops
and retreats. ✉*2 mi north of Mt. Carmel Junction on
U.S. 89, mile marker 84, Mt. Carmel* ☎*435/648–2653 or
801/533–5330* ⊕*www.thunderbirdfoundation.com* 💲*$20*
⊙*Tours by appointment only May–Oct., Mon.–Sat.*

WHERE TO STAY

$ ▣**Best Western East Zion Thunderbird Lodge.** A quick 13 mi
drive east of Zion National Park, this red-adobe motel is
a good option if lodging in Springdale has filled up or if
you want to be within an hour's drive of Bryce Canyon
National Park. Surrounded by the Zion Mountains and
bordered by a scenic golf course, the rooms are spacious
and bright. **Pros:** a convenient base for visiting Zion and
Bryce (and even the North Rim of the Grand Canyon).
Cons: no attractions within walking distance; restaurant
has good pies and does all of its own baking. ✉*Junction
of U.S. 89 and Rte. 9, Box 5531* ☎*435/648–2203 or
888/848–6358* ⊕*www.bestwestern.com* ⇄*62 rooms* ⏚*In-
room: kitchen (some), Internet, Wi-Fi. In-hotel: restaurant,
golf course, pool, spa, laundry facilities, Internet terminal,
no-smoking rooms* ⊟*AE, D, DC, MC, V.*

¢–$ ▣**Golden Hills Motel.** This clean and simple establishment
right at Mt. Carmel Junction is an inexpensive and no-frills

lodging option. Its funky pink-and-blue roadside diner serves good, basic country-style fare like country-fried steak, liver and onions, and homemade breads and pies. Some rooms in this ground-level facility are on the riverside. **Pros:** one of the most affordable lodgings in the vicinity of Zion National Park. **Cons:** reasonable prices mean you'll need to reserve early. ⊠*Junction of U.S. 89 and Rte. 9* ☎*435/648–2268 or 800/648–2268* ⊕*www.goldenhills motel.com* ⇴*30 rooms* ⚿*In-room: refrigerator, DVD (some), Wi-Fi. In-hotel: restaurant, pool, gym, bicycles, laundry facilities, Internet terminal, Wi-Fi, some pets allowed, no-smoking rooms* ⊟*MC, V.*

$$–
$$$$ 🖵**Zion Ponderosa Ranch Resort.** This multipursuit resort on a 4,000-acre ranch just east of Zion National Park offers activities from horseback riding to spa treatments, and just about everything in between. Lodging options range from camping to suites that sleep six and luxurious mountain homes for up to 13. **Pros:** a true mountain retreat on the "quiet" side of Zion National Park. **Cons:** tries to offer something for everyone from backpacker to luxury resort guest, well off the beaten path with no services close by. ⊠*5 mi north of route marker 46 on North Fork Country Rd., Mount Carmel* ☎*800/293–5444* ⊕*www.zionponde rosa.com* ⇴*16 suites, 8 cabins, 17 houses* ⚿*In-room: kitchen (some), DVD (some), Wi-Fi (some). In-hotel: restaurant, tennis courts, pool, spa, bicycles, children's programs (ages 4–11)* ⊟*AE, D, MC, V* Ⓞ*EP* ⊘*Closed Dec.–Feb.*

KANAB

17 mi southeast of Zion National Park (East entrance) via Rte. 9 and U.S. 89 south.

Kanab is Hollywood's vision of the American West. Soaring vermilion sandstone cliffs and sagebrush flats with endless vistas have lured filmmakers to this area for more than 75 years. The welcoming sign at city limits reads "Greatest Earth on Show"—Kanab has been used as a setting in more than 100 movies and television shows. Abandoned film sets have become tourist attractions, and old movie posters or still photographs are a decorating staple at local businesses. In addition to a movie-star past, Kanab is ideally positioned as a base for exploration. With major roads radiating in four directions, it offers easy access to three national parks, three national monuments (including

Grand Staircase–Escalante), two state parks, and several historic sites.

PIPE SPRING NATIONAL MONUMENT. In Arizona on the Kaibab-Paiute Reservation, Pipe Spring National Monument was established in 1923 as "a memorial of western pioneer life." Pipe Spring was a flashpoint for the convergence of Mormon settlers, the country's western expansion, and the Kaibab band of Paiute Indians. From Zion, exit the east side of the park. Turn south at Mt. Carmel Junction for 17 mi to Kanab. Pipe Spring is 22 mi southeast of Kanab.

WHAT TO SEE

Eroding sandstone formed the sweeping expanse of pink sand at **Coral Pink Sand Dunes State Park.** Funneled through a notch in the rock, the wind picks up speed and carries grains of sand into the area. Once the wind slows down, the sand is deposited, creating this giant playground for dune buggies, ATVs, and dirt bikes. A small area is fenced off for walking, but the sound of wheeled toys is always with you. Children love to play in the sand, but before you let them loose, check the surface temperature; it can become very hot. ⊠ *Yellowjacket and Hancock Rds., 12 mi off U.S. 89, near Kanab* ☎ *435/648–2800* ⊕ *www.stateparks.utah. gov* 🖃 *$6* ⊙ *Daily dawn–dusk.*

The main **Grand Staircase–Escalante Visitor Center** (⊠ *190 E. Center St., Kanab* ☎ *435/644–4300* ⊙ *Daily 8–5*) is in Kanab. It features exhibits on archaeology, the Monument's topography and geology. Bureau of Land Management staff are on hand year-round to answer questions and provide latest weather and conditions. If you're headed to the southwest corner of the monument, start here.

Housed in a replica of an ancient Native American cliff dwelling, **Moqui Cave** offers a little bit of everything. Native American artifacts are displayed alongside dinosaur footprints, a fluorescent mineral display, and pre-Columbian artifacts from Mexico, as well as a gift shop selling Indian jewelry. The inside temperature of the cave never exceeds 70°F, even on hot summer days. ⊠ *5½ mi north of Kanab on Utah U.S. 89* ☎ *435/644–8525* ⊕ *www.moquicave.com* ⊙ *May–Sept., Mon.–Sat. 9–7; Oct.–Apr., Mon.–Sat. 10–4.*

The nostalgic **Western Legends Roundup** (☎ *800/733–5263*) is for anyone who loves cowboys, pioneer life, or Native

8

American culture. For four days every August, Kanab fills with cowboy poets and storytellers, musicians, Western arts-and-crafts vendors, and Native American dancers and weavers.

WHERE TO EAT

$ ✕**Escobar's Mexican Restaurant.** *Mexican.* Brown vinyl booths line the turquoise-and-pink walls of this family-owned diner, which hums with the conversation of locals who flock here for the chili verde and steak ranchero. Cool the warm flavors with a cold bottle of beer, but don't touch the plates—they arrive piping hot. Breakfast is served from 11 AM to noon. ⊠*373 E. 300 South St.* ☎*435/644-3739* ⊟*MC, V* ⊘*Closed Sat.*

$ ✕**Fernando's Hideaway.** *Mexican.* Fernando's mixes the best margarita for miles—it's mighty fine with a quesadilla as a warm-up for dinner. The house salsa is chunky and fresh, and menu items are available as dinner platters or à la carte. Steaks and seafood will please those with a hankering for American food. Accommodations are made for vegetarians. Colorful Mexican folk art adorns the bright dining room, and the patio may encourage you to linger with another margarita. ⊠*332 N. 300 West St.* ☎*435/644-3222* ⊟*AE, MC, V* ⊘*Closed Oct.–mid-Feb.*

$$ ✕**Houston's Trail's End.** *American.* Servers wear cowboy shirts, denim, and holstered six-shooters (replicas, presumably) at this downtown eatery. Locals come for the steaks and other basics. Tasty country potatoes with onions and peppers are served with breakfast entrées. ⊠*32 E. Center St.* ☎*435/644-2488* ⊟*AE, D, DC, MC, V* ⊘*Closed Dec.–Feb.*

$$ ✕**Nedra's, Too.** *Mexican.* The first Nedra's restaurant was in Fredonia, Arizona, hence the name of this branch. Booths and tables, friendly service, and authentic Mexican specialties all come at a reasonable price. The menu also has sandwiches, soups, and desserts, and you can get breakfast here, too. ⊠*310 S. 100 East St.* ☎*435/644-2030* ⊟*AE, D, MC, V.*

$$–$$$ ✕**Rocking V Cafe.** *Contemporary.* Fresh fish, including mahi-
★ mahi when available, arrives several times a week at this respected café that prides itself on "slow food." Buffalo tenderloin is a favorite, but vegetarians and vegans have plenty of choices, as well. Save room for dessert—the crème brûlée is perfectly prepared. Lunch offers a more casual

selection of wraps, sandwiches, burgers, and salads. A full liquor license supports a decent wine and beer list, but cocktails are limited to standards such as margaritas. The Web site is a must-read—trust us. ⊠ *97 W. Center St.* ☎ *435/644–8001* ⊕ *www.rockingvcafe.com* ⊟ *MC, V* ⊗ *Closed Jan.–late Mar.*

¢ ╳ **Vermillion Espresso Bar & Café.** *Café.* If you like Internet access with your cup of coffee and pastry—or sandwich prepared on a croissant, bagel, or demi-baguette—this is the place for you. You can also relax on the sofa and choose from a selection of books and magazines littering the coffee table. The owner has been known to open early to accommodate tourists' schedules. ⊠ *4 E. Center St.* ☎ *435/ 644–3886* ⊟ *MC, V.*

WHERE TO STAY

$–$$ ▦ **Best Western Red Hills.** One of Kanab's larger motels has a hearty dose of cowboy flavor accenting its city-style amenities. The downtown shopping and dining district is only a few blocks away. **Pros:** within 30 minutes of Zion National Park, children under 17 stay free. **Cons:** no on-site restaurant. ⊠ *125 W. Center St.* ☎ *435/644–2675 or 800/830–2675* ⊕ *www.bestwesternredhills.com* ⊅ *75 rooms* ⟑ *In-room: refrigerator, Wi-Fi. In-hotel: pool, laundry facilities, Internet terminal, Wi-Fi, some pets allowed, no-smoking rooms* ⊟ *AE, D, MC, V* ⦿ *CP.*

$ ▦ **Parry Lodge.** The lobby of this colonial-style building, ★ constructed in 1929, is lined with photos of movie stars, including Ronald Reagan and Barbara Stanwyk, who stayed here while filming in the area. Some of the spacious rooms have plaques over the doors to tell you who stayed here before you. The lodge barn, which housed Victor Mature's camels during the making of *Timbuktu*, is now a playhouse, where old-time Western melodramas are performed in summer. **Pros:** film buffs will enjoy sleeping among the ghosts of Hollywood past. **Cons:** the dining room serves breakfast only from April through October. ⊠ *89 E. Center St.* ☎ *435/644–2601 or 888/289–1722* ⊕ *www.parrylodge. com* ⊅ *89 rooms* ⟑ *In-room: kitchen (some), Wi-Fi. In-hotel: restaurant, pool, laundry facilities, no-smoking rooms* ⊟ *AE, D, MC, V* ⊗ *Only open when there are reservations (which are required) Nov.–Mar.*

$–$$ ▦ **Shilo Inn.** On the outskirts of town, this two-story Western chain has updated minisuites done in soft pastels. The largest property in town, all rooms now feature microwaves and refrigerators. A shuttle to Kanab airport is available. **Pros:** updated rooms, complimentary Continental breakfast, convenient to area attractions. **Cons:** there are less expensive hotels in town, small pool. ⊠*296 W. 100 North St.* ☎*435/644–2562 or 800/222–2244* ⊕*www.shiloinns.com* ↪*117 rooms* ✦*In-room: microwave, refrigerator, Wi-Fi. In-hotel: pool, laundry facilities, no-smoking rooms, some pets allowed* ☐*AE, D, DC, MC, V* ⦿*CP.*

WHERE TO CAMP

$ ⚠**Coral Pink Sand Dunes Campground.** Close to Kanab, this small scenic campground tends to be less crowded than those at the nearby national parks. Be warned, however, that most of Coral Pink's campers are here to ride their ATVs, dune buggies, and motorcycles across the dunes. The campground is open all year, but there's no water from October until Easter. The sites are suitable for tents or RVs. ⊠*Yellowjacket and Hancock Rds., 12 mi off U.S. 89, near Kanab* ☎*435/648–2800, 800/322–3770 reservations* ↪*22 sites* ✦*Flush toilets, dump station, drinking water, showers, fire grates, picnic tables, ranger station.*

NIGHTLIFE & THE ARTS

☾ The **Crescent Moon Theater** (⊠*150 S. 100 East St.* ☎*435/ 644–2350*) performs Branson, Missouri–style entertainment with a Western twist six nights a week from May to October. The two-hour performance includes live music, as well as comedy and variety shows.

SHOPPING

Don't despair if your camera needs repair. Terry Alderman ★ of **Terry's Camera Trading Co.** (⊠*19 W. Center St.* ☎*435/ 644–5981*) will get you back out shooting in as little as two hours. While you wait, check out his immaculate used-and vintage-equipment selection that rivals that of big-city camera stores. If you're not careful you might just walk out with a Leica or a Hasselblad. An accomplished photographer for more than 40 years, Terry also holds photography workshops in the area's backcountry.

Saunter in and pick up a Stetson hat, genuine Indian jewelry, or a Navajo rug at **Denny's Wigwam** (⊠*78 E. Center St.* ☎*435/644–2452*). After shopping, get a coffee and homemade fudge to go.

PANGUITCH

24 mi northwest of Bryce via Rte. 12 and Rte. 89.

An elevation of 6,650 feet helps this town of 1,600 residents keep its cool. Main Street is lined with late-19th-century buildings, and its early homes and outbuildings are noted for their distinctive brick architecture. Decent amenities, inexpensive lodging (mainly strip motels), and an excellent location 24 mi northwest of Bryce Canyon National Park make Panguitch a comfortable launching pad for recreation in the area.

WHAT TO SEE

During late June, you can watch hot-air balloons float over canyon country during the **Panguitch Valley Balloon Rally** (☎*435/676–2514 or 866/590–4134*).

The old Panguitch High School, built in 1936, is still a place of learning. The taxidermy collection at the **Paunsagaunt Wildlife Museum** includes stuffed animals in tableaus mimicking actual terrain and animal behavior. The animals and birds come from all parts of the food chain. An African room has baboons, bush pigs, cape buffalo, and a lion. ✉*205 E. Center St.* ☎*435/676–2500* ⊕*www.brycecanyonwildlifemuseum.com* 💲*$2* ⊙*May–Nov., daily 9 AM–10 PM.*

During the bitter winter of 1864, Panguitch residents were on the verge of starvation. A group of men from the settlement set out over the mountains to fetch provisions from the town of Parowan, 40 mi away. When they hit waist-deep snowdrifts they were forced to abandon their oxen. Legend says the men, frustrated and ready to turn back, laid a quilt on the snow and knelt to pray. Soon they realized the quilt had kept them from sinking into the snow. Spreading quilts before them as they walked, leapfrog style, the men traveled to Parowan and back, returning with life-saving provisions. Every June, the four-day **Quilt Walk Festival** (☎*435/676–2418* ⊕*www.quiltwalk.com*) commemorates the event with quilting classes, a tour of Panguitch pioneer homes, crafts shows, and a dinner-theater production in which the story is acted out.

SPORTS & THE OUTDOORS

FISHING

Reportedly, **Panguitch Lake** takes its name from a Paiute Indian word meaning "big fish." They may not all be big, but several types of trout are plentiful, and ice fishing is popular in winter. Watch out that a bald eagle doesn't take your catch. ⊠*17 mi south of Panguitch on Rte. 143* ☎*435/676–2649* ⊕*www.panguitchlake.com.*

WHERE TO EAT & STAY

$ ✕**Bronco Bobbi's.** *Café.* For a real cup of coffee before your
★ early-morning adventures in Bryce Canyon, Bronco Bobbi's is open and serving fresh-brewed espresso-based drinks. Enjoy an eclectic selection of western wear, memorabilia, and jewelry while you wait. ⊠*37 N. Main St.* ☎*435/690–0044* ▭*MC, V* ⊗*Closed Sun.*

$–$$ ✕**Cowboy's Smokehouse Café.** *American.* Stuffed animal trophies and hundreds of business cards and photographs from customers line the walls at this barbecue joint. Specialties include mesquite-smoked beef, pork, turkey, and chicken, and a sauce with no fewer than 15 secret ingredients. Try the homemade peach, apricot, or cherry cobbler if you have room for dessert. Breakfast is served, too. ⊠*95 N. Main St.* ☎*435/676–8030* ▭*MC, V* ⊗*Closed Sun.*

$–$$ ▦**Marianna Inn Motel.** Rooms at this clean, family-friendly,
☾ one-story motel have up to four beds; those with whirlpool baths are $25 extra. You can barbecue your own supper on one of the grills and eat your meal on the covered patio. Relax afterward on a hammock or in the summer-only outdoor spa. **Pros:** distance from Bryce means reservations typically are easier to come by. **Cons:** some may find Panguitch too sleepy. ⊠*699 N. Main St.* ☎*435/676–8844* ⊕*www.mariannainn.com* ↪*32 rooms* ☾*In-room: refrigerator (some). In-hotel: some pets allowed, no-smoking rooms* ▭*AE, D, DC, MC, V.*

¢ ▦**Panguitch Inn.** This quiet inn occupies a 100-year-old, two-story building a few blocks from downtown restaurants and shops. Rooms are simple and no-frills. **Pros:** Covered indoor parking. **Cons:** Rooms don't match building's quaintness. ⊠*50 N. Main St.* ☎*435/676–8871* ⊕*www. panguitchinn.com* ↪*25 rooms* ☾*In-room: Wi-Fi. In-hotel: no-smoking rooms* ▭*AE, D, DC, MC, V* ⊗*Closed Nov.–Mar.*

WHERE TO CAMP

$ ⛺**White Bridge Campground.** About 30 mi from Bryce Canyon on the way to Cedar Breaks National Monument, this alpine meadow campground is primitive but will satisfy those seeking a quiet camping experience. Panguitch Creek trickles nearby and Panguitch Lake is 4 mi away. All of the sites are suitable for tents or RVs. ✉ *12 mi southwest of Panguitch on Rte. 143* ☎ *435/865–3700* ⊕ *www.fs.fed.us/ r4/dixie* 🛏 *29 sites* ♿ *Flush toilets, drinking water, fire grates* ⊙ *May or June (weather permitting)–Oct.*

SHOPPING

Dusty old boots in need of a cowhand sit ready to walk and ride again at **Cowboy Collectibles** (✉ *21 N. Main St.* ☎ *435/676–8060*). The owners travel all over the country to find saddles, chaps, and other antiques from the days when men on horseback roamed the ranges. There are also toys and other products that celebrate the Old West. Why not pick up a 19th-century buffalo fur coat for $750?

GRAND STAIRCASE–ESCALANTE NATIONAL MONUMENT

In September 1996, President Bill Clinton designated 1.7 million acres in south-central Utah as the Grand Staircase–Escalante National Monument. Its three distinct sections—the Grand Staircase, the Kaiparowits Plateau, and the Canyons of the Escalante—offer remote back-country experiences hard to find elsewhere in the Lower 48. Waterfalls, Native American ruins and petroglyphs, shoulder-width slot canyons, and improbable colors all characterize this wilderness. Straddling the northern border of the monument, the small towns of Escalante and Boulder offer access, information, outfitters, lodging, and dining to adventurers. The highway that connects them, Route 12, is one of the most scenic stretches of road in the Southwest.

The Grand Staircase features five unique geological zones ranging from one billion years old (Chocolate Cliffs north of Grand Canyon) to 65 million years old (the Pink Cliffs of Bryce). Nearby, the Vermillion Cliffs (Kayenta formation), White Cliffs (Navajo sandstone), and Gray Cliffs (Dakota formation) contain dinosaur fossils, ancient lakebeds, and evidence of a massive arid desert—clues to our planet's geological history. To the modern day explorer, the national vast lands included in the national monument offer myriad slot canyons, cliff faces to climb, fantastic formations and much more.

The Kaiparowits Plateau is a rugged plateau due east of Bryce Canyon that provides refuge to hardy animals, rare plants, and uncompromising wilderness. With limited towns, roads, and services, this is a beautiful, but dangerous area. ■TIP➔**Make sure your gas tank is full and you have plenty of clearance in your (ideally) high-profile 4X4 vehicle.** Grosvenor Arch, one of the tallest natural arches in the world, is accessible by an 11-mi dirt road just south of Kodachrome Basin State Park.

The Canyons of the Escalante are cut by the Escalante River and its tributaries. Named for the Spanish explorer Father Silvestre Velez de Escalante (who incidentally never saw it), this region was first explored and mapped by John Wesley Powell. The towns of Escalante and Boulder are the best bases from which to explore the labyrinth of canyons, petrified forests, and Anasazi cultural sites.

ESCALANTE

47 mi east of Bryce Canyon National Park entrance via Rte. 12 east.

Though the Dominguez and Escalante expedition of 1776 came nowhere near this area, the town's name does honor the Spanish explorer. It was bestowed nearly a century later by a member of a survey party led by John Wesley Powell, charged with mapping this remote area. These days Escalante has modern amenities and is a western gateway to the Grand Staircase–Escalante National Monument.

Created to protect a huge repository of fossilized wood and dinosaur bones, **Escalante Petrified Forest State Park** has two short interpretive trails to educate visitors. There's an attractive swimming beach at the park's Wide Hollow Reservoir, which is also good for boating, fishing, and birding. ⊠*710 N. Reservoir Rd.* ☎*435/826–4466* ⊕*www. stateparks.utah.gov* ⊠*$5* ⊙*Daily 8* AM–*10* PM.

★ FodorsChoice Keep your camera handy and steering wheel steady along **Highway 12 Scenic Byway** between Escalante and Loa, near Capitol Reef National Park. Though the highway starts at the intersection of U.S. 89, west of Bryce Canyon National Park, the stretch that begins in Escalante is one of the most spectacular. The road passes through Grand Staircase–Escalante National Monument and on to Capitol Reef along one of the most scenic stretches of highway in the United States. Be sure to stop at the scenic overlooks; almost every one will give you an eye-popping view. Don't get distracted, though; the paved road is twisting and steep, and at times climbs over a hogback with sheer drop-offs on both sides.

SPORTS & THE OUTDOORS

Larger than most national parks at 1.7 million acres, the Grand Staircase–Escalante National Monument is popular with backpackers and hard-core mountain bike enthusiasts. You can explore the rocky landscape, which represents some of America's last wilderness, via dirt roads with a four-wheel-drive vehicle; most roads depart from Route 12. Roadside views into the monument are most impressive from Route 12 between Escalante and Boulder. It costs nothing to enter the park, but fees apply for camping and backcountry permits.

VISITOR CENTERS

Contact the **Escalante Interagency Visitor Center** (⊠ *755 W. Main St.* ☎ *435/826–5499* ⊕ *www.ut.blm.gov/monument* ⊗ *Mid-Mar.–mid-Nov., daily 7:30–5:30; mid-Nov.–mid-Mar., weekdays 8–4:30*) for permits and detailed information.

A new **Grand Staircase–Escalante Visitor's Center** (⊠ *10 Center St., Cannonville* ☎ *435/826–5640* ⊕ *www.ut.blm.gov/monument* ⊗ *Mar.–Nov., daily 8–4:30*) has indoor and outdoor exhibits about the national monument. The staff can answer your questions and offer the latest weather and road conditions. You can also purchase maps, books, and souvenirs here. Head southwest to Sheep Creek and Willits Creek hikes, or east to Kodachrome Basin State Park, Grosvenor Arch, and Cottonwood Road.

Canyoneering and hiking are the focus of **Excursions of Escalante,** where tours are custom-fit to your schedule and needs. All necessary gear is provided, and tours last from one to eight days. ⊠ *125 E. Main St.* ☎ *800/839–7567* ⊕ *www.excursions-escalante.com* ⊗ *Wed.–Mon. 8–5 or by appointment.*

Hondoo Rivers & Trails (⊠ *95 E. Main St., Box 98, Torrey* ☎ *435/425–3519 or 800/332–2696* ⊕ *www.hondoo.com*) arranges full-day four-wheel-drive vehicle tours into portions of the Grand Staircase–Escalante National Monument.

BICYCLING

A good long-distance mountain-bike ride in the isolated Escalante region follows the 44-mi **Hell's Backbone Road** from Escalante to Boulder. The grade is steep and, if you're driving, a four-wheel-drive vehicle is recommended, but the views of Box Death Hollow make it all worthwhile. The road leaves from the center of town. Inquire about road conditions before departing.

HIKING

Some of the best backcountry hiking in the area lies 15 mi east of Escalante on Route 12, where the **Lower Escalante River** carves through striking sandstone canyons and gulches. You can camp at numerous sites along the river for extended trips, or you can spend a little time in the small park where the highway crosses the river.

With a guided tour from **Utah Canyons** (⊠*325 W. Main St.* ☎*435/826–4967* ⊕*www.utahcanyons.com*), you can slip into the slot canyons with confidence or end a day of adventure by watching a sunset from the rim of a canyon.

WHERE TO EAT & STAY

¢–$ ✕**Esca-Latte Coffee Shop & Cafe.** *Café.* Fuel up for your hike with the best coffee in town. When you're hot and spent after your day of exploration, there's no better place to sit back and relax with friends. Try a turkey sub or homemade pizza with a cold draft microbrew, or opt for a salad. Watch hummingbirds fight the wind at the feeders while dining on the patio. ⊠*310 W. Main St.* ☎*435/826–4266* ▭*AE, D, MC, V.*

$$ ⬚**Escalante's Grand Staircase Bed & Breakfast Inn.** Rooms have
★ skylights, tile floors, log furniture, and murals reproducing area petroglyphs. You can relax on the outdoor porches or in the library, or make use of the rental bikes to explore the adjacent national monument. **Pro:** Southwestern rusticity with modern flair. **Con:** Escalante's wonderful remoteness may not be for everyone. ⊠*280 W. Main St., Box 657, Escalante* ☎*435/826–4890 or 866/826–4890* ⊕*www.escalantebnb.com* ⇌*8 rooms* ◊*In-room: no a/c, no phone, no TV, Wi-Fi. In-hotel: no elevator, public Wi-Fi, no kids under 12, no-smoking rooms* ▭*AE, D, MC, V* ⦶*BP.*

Travel Smart
Zion & Bryce
Canyon National
Parks

WORD OF MOUTH

"Last year I purchased a Senior Lifetime National Park pass. Once again it got considerable use as we visited four National Parks."

—Myer

GETTING HERE & AROUND

We're proud of our Web site: Fodors.com is a great place to begin any journey. Scan Travel Wire for suggested itineraries, travel deals, restaurant and hotel openings, and other up-to-the-minute info. Check out Booking to research prices and book plane tickets, hotel rooms, rental cars, and vacation packages. Head to Talk for on-the-ground pointers from travelers who frequent our message boards. You can also link to loads of other travel-related resources.

Separated by about 90 mi (along two-lane scenic Highway 89), Zion and Bryce Canyon national parks attract millions of visitors annually despite their remote locations. Plan on at least three to five hours of driving from the closest major airports (Las Vegas and Salt Lake City), but savor the time spent on some of the Southwest's most memorable scenic drives. Weather and elevation are two important considerations here. In summer, flash floods and incendiary heat (well over 110°F at low elevations in summer) can be real perils. In winter, many back roads at the higher elevations are impassable due to snow and/or extreme cold. Travel by horseback, bicycle, ATV, 4X4, and other means can be thrilling adventures, but be aware that natural elements can be deadly for the unprepared traveler. Gas stations in this part of the country may be more than 100 mi apart—and many places in this heavily Mor-

mon part of the state are closed on Sunday.

Package deals in this region may include skiing, Shakespearean theater, golf, backcountry adventures, and/or local cultural festivals.

▌ BY AIR

The major gateway to Utah is Salt Lake City International Airport, but a more convenient gateway to southern Utah, particularly if you're going only to Zion and Bryce Canyon national parks, is McCarran International Airport in Las Vegas. Booming St. George's small airport is served by daily flights on several airlines from Salt Lake City, Las Vegas, Phoenix, and other western cities.

Airlines & Airports **Airline and Airport Links.com** (⊕ *www.airline andairportlinks.com*) has links to many of the world's airlines and airports.

Airline Security Issues **Transportation Security Administration** (⊕ *www.tsa.gov*) has answers for almost every question that might come up.

AIRPORTS
Both Salt Lake City and McCarran airports are big, busy hubs. In McCarran security can take a long time.

Airport Information **McCarran International Airport (LAS)** (☎ *702/261–5211* ⊕ *www.mccarran.*

com). **Salt Lake City International Airport (SLC)** (☎801/575–2400 ⊕www.slcairport.com).

FLIGHTS

Salt Lake City has a large international airport, so you'll be able to fly here from anywhere in the United States. The airport is the major Western hub for Delta Airlines, which connects to the world through Atlanta and Minneapolis. Southwest Airlines and jetBlue also have major presences here and may offer great fares, if not as many daily flights.

You may find it more convenient to fly into Las Vegas, which has more flights and is often a cheaper destination. Connecting flights to St. George and Cedar City may be available from either Salt Lake or Las Vegas, though it's often just as easy (and cheaper) to drive.

Airline Contacts **American Airlines** (☎800/433–7300 ⊕www. aa.com).**Continental Airlines** (☎800/523–3273 for U.S. and Mexico reservations, 800/231–0856 for international reservations ⊕www. continental.com). **Delta Airlines** (☎800/221–1212 for U.S. reservations, 800/241–4141 for international reservations ⊕www.delta. com). **Frontier** (☎800/432–1359 ⊕www.frontierairlines.com). **jetBlue** (☎800/538–2583 ⊕www. jetblue.com). **Northwest Airlines** (☎800/225–2525 ⊕www.nwa. com). **SkyWest** (☎800/453–9417 ⊕www.skywest.com). **Southwest Airlines** (☎800/435–9792 ⊕www. southwest.com). **United Airlines** (☎800/864–8331 for U.S. reservations, 800/538–2929 for international reservations ⊕www.united. com). **USAirways** (☎800/428–4322 for U.S. and Canada reservations, 800/622–1015 for international reservations ⊕www.usairways.com).

▌ BY CAR

You will need a car to get to Zion and Bryce, but you'll seldom be bored driving. Scenery ranges from snow-capped mountains to endless stretches of desert with strange rock formations and intense color. There are more national parks in Utah than in any other state except Alaska and California, although their interiors are not always accessible by car.

Before setting out on any driving trip, it's important to make sure your vehicle is in top condition. It is best to have a complete tune-up. At the least, you should check the following: lights, including brake lights, backup lights, and emergency lights; tires, including the spare; oil; engine coolant; windshield-washer fluid; windshield-wiper blades; and brakes. For emergencies, take along flares or reflector triangles, jumper cables, an empty gas can, a fire extinguisher, a flashlight, a plastic tarp, blankets, water, and coins or a calling card for phone calls (cell phones don't always work in high mountain areas).

GASOLINE

In cities like St. George and Cedar City, gas prices are roughly similar to the rest of the continental United States. In rural and resort towns, and in remote stretches of I–15 or I–70, prices can be considerably higher. In urban areas, stations are plentiful, and most stay open late (some are open 24 hours). In rural areas, stations are less frequent, and hours are more limited, particularly on Sunday; you can sometimes drive more than 100 mi on back roads without finding gas. It's best to always keep your tank at least half full.

Area Service Stations **Bryce Canyon Towing** (⊠1 mi north of park on Rte. 63, Bryce ☎435/834–5232). **Canyon Tire** (962 Zion Park Blvd., Springdale ☎435/772–3963). **Chevron at Ruby's Inn** (⊠Rte. 63, 1 mi north of park entrance, Bryce ☎435/834–5484). **Kanab Tire Center** (⊠265 E. 300 South St., Kanab ☎435/644–2557). **Springdale Chevron** (⊠1593 Zion Park Blvd., Springdale ☎435/772–3922). **Zion's Sinclair** (⊠Rte. 9, at east entrance to Zion National Park, Orderville ☎435/648–2828).

RENTAL CARS
You can rent an economy car with air-conditioning, an automatic transmission, and unlimited mileage in Salt Lake City for about $30 a day and $150 a week. This does not include tax on car rentals, which is 16.35% in Salt Lake City. If you're planning to do any skiing, biking, four-wheeling, or towing, check into renting an SUV, van, or pickup from a local company like Rugged Rentals, which specializes in outdoor vehicles and provides supplemental insurance as part of the rental charge. For around $60 per day or $300 per week (plus taxes and other fees), you can rent a relatively new SUV

or van with bike rack, ski rack, or towing equipment included.

Renting a car in Las Vegas can be less expensive than renting one in Salt Lake City, especially if you're visiting southern Utah. The driving time between Las Vegas and Salt Lake City is seven to nine hours, but it's only a two- to three-hour trip from Las Vegas to Zion National Park.

In Utah you must be 21 and have a valid driver's license to rent a car; most companies also require a major credit card. If you're over 65, check the rental company's policy on overage drivers. You may pay extra for child seats (but shop around; some companies don't charge extra for this), which are compulsory for children under five, and for additional drivers. Non-U.S. residents will need a reservation voucher, a passport, a driver's license, and a travel policy that covers each driver, in order to pick up a car.

Contacts **Alamo** (☎800/462–5266 ⊕www.alamo.com). **Avis** (☎800/462–5266 ⊕www.avis.com). **Budget** (☎800/527–0700 ⊕www.budget.com). **Hertz** (☎800/654–3131 ⊕www.hertz.com). **National** (☎800/227–7368 ⊕www.nationalcar.com).

RENTAL CAR INSURANCE
Everyone who rents a car wonders whether the insurance that the rental companies offer is worth the expense. No one—including us—has a simple answer. If you own a car, your personal auto insurance may cover a rental to some degree, though not all policies protect you

abroad; always read your policy's fine print. If you don't have auto insurance, then seriously consider buying the collision- or loss-damage waiver (CDW or LDW) from the car-rental company, which eliminates your liability for damage to the car. Some credit cards offer CDW coverage, but it's usually supplemental to your own insurance and rarely covers SUVs, minivans, luxury models, and the like. If your coverage is secondary, you may still be liable for loss-of-use costs from the car-rental company. But no credit-card insurance is valid unless you use that card for *all* transactions, from reserving to paying the final bill. All companies exclude car rental in some countries, so be sure to find out about the destination to which you are traveling. It's sometimes cheaper to buy insurance as part of your general travel insurance policy.

ROADSIDE EMERGENCIES

Throughout Utah, call 911 for any travel emergency, such as an accident or a serious health concern. For automotive breakdowns, 911 is not appropriate. Instead, find a local directory and dial a towing service. When out on the open highway, call the nonemergency central administration phone number of the Utah Highway Patrol for assistance.

Emergency Services **Utah Highway Patrol** (☎ *801/965–4518* ⊕ *highwaypatrol.utah.gov*).

ROAD CONDITIONS

Utah has some of the most spectacular vistas—and challenging driving—in the world. Roads range from multilane blacktop to narrow dirt roads; from twisting switchbacks bordered by guardrails to primitive backcountry paths so narrow that you must back up to the edge of a steep cliff to make a turn. Scenic routes and lookout points are clearly marked, enabling you to slow down and pull over to take in the views. You can find highways and the national parks crowded in summer, and almost deserted (and occasionally impassable) in winter. Deer, elk, and even bears may try to get to the other side of a road just as you come along, so watch out for wildlife on the highways. One of the more unpleasant frequent sights along the highway are road kills—animals struck by vehicles. Exercise caution, not only to save an animal's life, but also to avoid possible extensive damage to your car.

Road Conditions **In Utah** (☎ *511* ⊕ *commuterlink.utah.gov*).

▌ BY TRAIN

Amtrak has some service to Las Vegas, Salt Lake City, and St. George.

Contacts **Amtrak** (☎ *800/872-7245* ⊕ *www.amtrak.com*).

ESSENTIALS

▌ ACCESSIBILITY

In Zion, both visitor centers, all shuttle buses, and Zion Lodge are fully accessible to wheelchairs. Several campsites (sites A24 and A25 at Watchman Campground; sites 103, 114, and 115 at South Campground) are reserved for people with disabilities, and two trails—Riverside Walk and Pa'rus Trail—are accessible with some assistance.

In Bryce, most park facilities were constructed between 1930 and 1960. Some have been upgraded to increase accessibility for travelers with disabilities, while others can be used with some assistance. Because of the park's natural terrain, only a ½-mi section of the Rim Trail between Sunset and Sunrise points is wheelchair-accessible. The 1-mi Bristlecone Loop Trail at Rainbow Point has a hard surface and could be used with assistance, but several grades do not meet standards. Handicapped parking is marked at all overlooks and public facilities. Accessible campsites are available at Sunset Campground.

▌ ADMISSION FEES

Entrance to Zion National Park is $25 per vehicle for a seven-day pass, which includes the Kolob Canyons section, which has a separate entrance. People entering on foot or by bicycle or motorcycle pay $12 per person (not to exceed $25 per family) for a seven-day pass. An annual pass for Zion Canyon National Park, good for one year from the date of purchase, costs $30.

The entrance fee for Bryce Canyon National Park is $25 per vehicle for a seven-day pass and $12 for pedestrians, bicyclists, or motorcyclists. An annual pass for Bryce Canyon National Park, good for one year from the date of purchase, costs $30. This pass can also be used on the park shuttle. If you leave your private vehicle outside the park, the one-time entrance fee, including transportation on the shuttle, is $12.

▌ COMMUNICATIONS

INTERNET

Most major chain hotels and many smaller motels throughout Utah now offer Wi-Fi or other Internet access at no cost to guests. Many coffee shops provide free Wi-Fi (although it's a little harder to find in southern Utah), as do most libraries, which also provide computers with Internet access. Contacts **Cybercafes** (⊕ *www. cybercafes.com*).

PHONES

The area code in Zion and Bryce Canyon is 435. Cellular service is generally available along I–15 in central Utah and in the vicinity of both park's main visitor centers. St. George and Cedar City have strong coverage, but the mountainous terrain can make it spotty in places.

Coverage will be patchy everywhere else in southern Utah.

EMERGENCIES

In the event of an emergency, dial 911, report to a visitor center, or contact a park ranger.

In Zion National Park you can reach a park ranger at ☎435/772–3322. The nearest hospitals are in St. George, Cedar City, and Kanab, but Zion Canyon Medical Clinic is open from June through late September, Monday to Saturday from 9 to 5, and accepts walk-in patients.

In Bryce Canyon National Park, there is also first aid at Bryce Canyon Lodge, though only in the summer months. The nearest hospital is in Panguitch.

Emergency Services **Ambulance, police** (☎911).

Clinics & Hospitals **Garfield Memorial Hospital** (⊠200 N. 400 East St., Panguitch ☎435/676–8811). **Zion Canyon Medical Clinic** (⊠120 Zion Blvd., Springdale ☎435/772–3226 ☉Mid-May–mid-Oct., Tues.–Sat. 9–5) accepts walk-in patients.

HOURS OF OPERATION

Both Zion and Bryce Canyon national parks are open daily year-round, 24 hours a day. Both are in the Mountain time zone.

LOST & FOUND

In both parks, the lost-and-found is at the main park visitor center.

MAIL

In Zion, you can mail letters and buy stamps at Zion Lodge, but the nearest full-service post office is in Springdale.

In Bryce, you can mail letters and buy stamps from Bryce Canyon National Park Lodge. Ruby's Inn also offers a full-service post office.

Post Offices **Ruby's Inn Post Office** (⊠Rte. 63, 1 mi north of park entrance, Bryce ☎435/834–8088 ☉Weekdays 9–5, Sat. 9–5, Sun. 10–4). **Springdale Post Office** (⊠625 Zion Park Blvd., Springdale☎800/275–8777).

MONEY

Zion National Park has no ATM, but there is a bank in Springdale with an ATM.

There is no ATM in Bryce Canyon National Park, but Ruby's Inn has an ATM. The nearest bank is in Panguitch.

Contacts **Ruby's Inn** (⊠Rte. 63, 1 mi north of park entrance, Bryce ☎435/834–5341) . **Zions Bank Panguitch** (⊠90 E. Center St., Panguitch ☎435/676–8855). **Zions Bank Springdale** (⊠921 Zion Park Blvd., Springdale☎435/772–3274).

CREDIT CARDS
Throughout this guide, the following abbreviations are used: **AE,** American Express; **D,** Discover; **DC,** Diners Club; **MC,** Master-Card; and **V,** Visa.

Reporting Lost Cards **American Express** (☎800/528–4800 ⊕www. americanexpress.com). **MasterCard**

(☎*800/627–8372* ⊕*www.master
card.com*). Visa (☎*800/847–2911*
⊕*www.visa.com*).

PERMITS

In Zion, permits are required for
backcountry camping and overnight climbs. The maximum size
of a group hiking into the backcountry is 12 people. The cost for
a permit for 1 to 2 people is $10;
for 3 to 7 people, $15; and for 8
to 12 people, $20. Permits and hik-
ing information are available at the
Zion Canyon Visitor Center.

In Bryce, a $5 backcountry permit,
available from the visitor center, is
required for camping in the park's
interior, allowed only on Under-
the-Rim Trail and Riggs Spring
Loop, both south of Bryce Point.
Campfires are not permitted.

RELIGIOUS SERVICES

In Zion, interdenominational ser-
vices are held in summer at Zion
Lodge and South Campground.
Check bulletin boards at the Zion
Canyon Visitor Center for times.

In Bryce, nondenominational and
Mormon services are held at Bryce
Canyon National Park Lodge.
Check bulletin boards at the vis-
itor center for times.

RESTROOMS

In Zion, public restrooms are at
the Grotto, Kolob Canyons Visitor
Center, Temple of Sinawava, Weeping Rock Trailhead, Zion Canyon
Visitor Center, Zion Human History Museum, and Zion Lodge.

In Bryce, there are public restrooms
at Bryce Canyon National Park
Lodge, Bryce Canyon Pines General Store, the south end of North
Campground, Ruby's General
Store, Ruby's Inn, Sunset Campground, Sunset Point, the visitor
center, and Yovimpa Point.

SAFETY

Threats in Zion and Bryce Canyon
national parks range from the lack
of preparedness to over exertion—
but regardless can be deadly. On
a backcountry hike, for example,
rangers in summer will warn you
about heat stroke, dehydration,
disorientation, flash floods, cougars, bears, lightning, rattlesnakes,
and undoubtedly a few other hazards. In winter, hypothermia and
blizzards are the biggest dangers.

But threats are just as real in the
frontcountry. Every year, day visitors slip on rocks, trip on uneven
surfaces, become dehydrated, suf-
fer from too much sun and/or have
heart and/or breathing problems
due to the extreme altitude at these
parks. Use common sense, know
your limitations and don't be afraid
to ask for help before it's too late.

In fact, Bryce publishes the top
10 causes for injuries in the park,
and some perhaps not unsurpris-
ing hazards come out at the top
of their list, including unsafe driving, climbing or skiing off the canyon rim, feeding animals, ignoring
extreme weather, dehydration, leav-
ing the trail, over-exhaustion, and
choosing the wrong footwear.

Call ☎*911* in either park for
emergencies. In Zion, call ☎*435/*

772–3322 to reach an on-duty ranger at any time. In Bryce, call ☎435/676–2411.

▮ TAXES

Sales tax is 4.65% in Utah and applies to everything, including food, but the percentage is somewhat less on nonprepared (grocery) food. Most areas have additional local sales and lodging taxes, which can be quite significant. For example, in Salt Lake City, the combined sales tax is 6.80%.

▮ TELEPHONES

In Zion, public telephones can be found at South Campground, Watchman Campground, Zion Canyon Visitor Center, Zion Lodge, and Zion Museum. Cell-phone reception is decent in Springdale but spotty in Zion Canyon itself.

In Bryce, public telephones can be found at Bryce Canyon National Park Lodge, Bryce Canyon Pines General Store, Ruby's Inn, Sunset Campground, and the visitor center. Cell-phone reception generally is available along the 18-mi drive.

▮ TIPPING

Utahans are notoriously stingy tippers, so don't ask a local what to tip. It's customary to tip 15% at restaurants, but 18% to 20% in resort towns is increasingly the norm. For coat checks and bell-hops, $1 per coat or bag is the minimum. Taxi drivers expect 10% to 15%, depending on where you are. In resort towns, ski technicians,

sandwich makers, coffee baristas, and the like also appreciate tips.

▮ TRIP INSURANCE

Comprehensive travel policies typically cover trip-cancellation and interruption, letting you cancel or cut your trip short because of a personal emergency, illness, or, in some cases, acts of terrorism in your destination. Such policies also cover evacuation and medical care. Some also cover you for trip delays because of bad weather or mechanical problems as well as for lost or delayed baggage. Another type of coverage to look for is financial default—that is, when your trip is disrupted because a tour operator, airline, or cruise line goes out of business. Generally you must buy this when you book your trip or shortly thereafter, and it's only available to you if your operator isn't on a list of excluded companies.

At the very least, consider buying medical-only coverage. Neither Medicare nor some private insurers cover medical expenses anywhere outside of the United States (including time aboard a cruise ship, even if it leaves from a U.S. port). Medical-only policies typically reimburse you for medical care (excluding that related to preexisting conditions) and hospitalization abroad, and provide for evacuation. You still have to pay the bills and await reimbursement from the insurer, though. Another option is to sign up with a medical-evacuation assistance company. A membership in one of these companies gets you doctor referrals, emergency evacuation or repatriation, 24-hour hotlines for medical consultation, and other assistance.

International SOS Assistance Emergency and AirMed International provide evacuation services and medical referrals. MedjetAssist offers medical evacuation. Expect comprehensive travel insurance policies to cost about 4% to 7% or 8% of the total price of your trip (it's more like 8%–12% if you're over age 70). A medical-only policy may or may not be cheaper than a comprehensive policy. Always read the fine print of your policy to make sure that you're covered for the risks that are of most concern to you. Compare several policies to make sure you're getting the best price and range of coverage available.

Insurance Comparison Sites **Insure My Trip.com** (☎800/487–4722 ⊕www.insuremytrip.com). **Square Mouth.com** (☎800/240–0369 or 727/490–5803 ⊕www.squaremouth.com).

Comprehensive Travel Insurers **Access America** (☎866/729–6021 ⊕www.accessamerica.com). **AIG Travel Guard** (☎800/826–4919 ⊕www.travelguard.com). **CSA Travel Protection** (☎800/873–9855 ⊕www.csatravelprotection.com). **HTH Worldwide** (☎610/254–8700 ⊕www.hthworldwide.com). **Travelex Insurance** (☎888/228–9792 ⊕www.travelex-insurance.com). **Travel Insured International** (☎800/243–3174 ⊕www.travel insured.com).

▎ VISITOR INFORMATION

Contacts **Bryce Canyon National Park** (☎435/834–5322 ⊕www.nps.gov/brca) **Zion National Park** (☎435/772–3256 ⊕www.nps.gov/zion).

INDEX

NOTES

NOTES

NOTES